Governance and Democracy in Africa

Governance and Democracy in Africa

Regional and Continental Perspectives

James S. Guseh

Emmanuel O. Oritsejafor

LEXINGTON BOOKS

Lanham • Boulder • New York • London

Published by Lexington Books
An imprint of The Rowman & Littlefield Publishing Group, Inc.
4501 Forbes Boulevard, Suite 200, Lanham, Maryland 20706
www.rowman.com

6 Tinworth Street, London SE11 5AL, United Kingdom

British Library Cataloguing in Publication Information Available

Library of Congress Cataloging-in-Publication Data Available

Names: Guseh, James S., author. | Oritsejafor, Emannuel O., author.
Title: Governance and democracy in Africa : regional and continental perspectives / James Guseh and Emmanuel Oritsejafor.
Description: Lanham : Lexington Books, 2019. | Includes bibliographical references and index.
Identifiers: LCCN 2018047644 (print) | LCCN 2018048614 (ebook) | ISBN 9781498533003 (electronic) | ISBN 9781498532990 (cloth : alk. paper)
Subjects: LCSH: Democracy—Africa—History. | Economic development—Africa—History. | Africa—Politics and government—1960- | Africa—Economic conditions—1960-
Classification: LCC JQ1879.A15 (ebook) | LCC JQ1879.A15 G87 2019 (print) | DDC 320.96—dc23
LC record available at https://lccn.loc.gov/2018047644

∞™ The paper used in this publication meets the minimum requirements of American National Standard for Information Sciences—Permanence of Paper for Printed Library Materials, ANSI/NISO Z39.48-1992.

Contents

Preface

Democratic governance has long been considered the best form of government for promoting human welfare and prosperity. For more than a half century, African countries have embarked on democratic governance. The purpose of this book, *Democracy and Governance in Africa*, is to provide a comprehensive and the most up-to-date assessment of the practice of democracy in Africa. Some of the issues discussed include "What has been the democratic trend in Africa for the past half century and what has been the benefit of democratic institutions?"

Studies have indicated that economies of countries with democratic institutions tend to grow faster than those in which this freedom is proscribed or circumscribed. We test this theory in the case of Africa. We are also cognizant of the opposition to this theory by some scholars and policy analysts who have argued that the economies of some nondemocratic socialist countries, such as China, have grown faster than those of many Western industrialized democracies. We assess this debate in our analysis.

As we embarked on completing this work, we began to realize the challenges we thought would make it difficult to complete the work. The success and decline of democracy on the continent made our task analogous to "shifting the goal post." We found that the goal post would shift when our findings of free and fair elections in some countries and authoritarian regimes in others would reverse within a short period. The state of democracy presented in this book for some countries may have changed by the time you read the book.

In writing this book we bring about thirty years of experience living and working in Africa and other parts of the world. We have held senior policy positions in government and have served as consultants to both governments and international organizations in Côte d'Ivoire, Ghana, Liberia, Nigeria, Rwanda, Sierra Leone, and South Africa. We have also served as professors in American universities for decades, where we have taught a wide range of courses and have produced many publications on Africa.

Acknowledgments

We are grateful to Omar Reyes, Arlena Nwosu, and Alan Cooper for their thorough and insightful reading of several drafts. We thank our wives, Thelma and Emma, and our families for their loving support. This book is for them.

Chapter 1

Introduction to Democratic Governance

Determining the best political and economic institutions for economic development is a quintessential issue in human history. In other words, what type of political and economic institutions can best address the central human concerns of development? Prior to the early 1990s, the world was characterized by two major modes of development—socialism, led by the former Soviet Union, and capitalism, led by the United States. Karl Marx, the proponent of socialism, predicted the collapse of capitalism and the expansion of socialism and communism in the twentieth century. On the other hand, Adam Smith, the founder of free market capitalism, stated that when each person makes the best economic choice based on self-interest, that choice leads as if by "an invisible hand" to the best outcome for society as a whole.[1]

During the 1990s the Soviet Union collapsed, breaking up into various independent states and leading to the demise of socialism. Since then, democratic capitalism has been flourishing across the globe and has accelerated through the process of globalization. Although globalization has been occurring for millennia, the term came to prominence in the 1980s. Globalization has been defined in terms of the interaction and integration between people, companies, and governments of different nations, a process driven by international trade and investment and aided by information technology.[2] This process affects the environment, culture, political systems, economic development and prosperity, and human physical well-being in societies around the world. The flourishing of democratic market institutions across the globe can be seen as the wave of political and economic globalization with many governments adopting democratic political and free market economic institutions.

Empirical studies have found that the economies of countries with democratic market institutions tend to perform better or grow faster than countries in which these freedoms are proscribed. Thus, economic growth can be influenced by the type of political institution. According to Berry, Conkling, and Ray,

> Centrally directed socialist systems do not work and cannot compete. They produce only sporadic growth, assure only a low-level equality that is violated by party-membership privilege, and quite demonstrably have been far more destructive of the environment than political and economic systems of any other kind.[3]

Democratic capitalism has proven to be the best institution for promoting economic growth and human welfare as well as laying the foundation for sustainable development. Countries, therefore, are abandoning socialist institutions and adopting democratic market institutions. Thus, we see the globalization of democratic market institutions flourishing from Eastern Europe to Asia, South America, and Africa. Extending this perspective, Plumer and Martin found that an increase in democracy leads to an increase in economic growth.[4] Another study went further to estimate the impact of democracy on economic growth in the long run. The study found that "a country that switches from no democracy to democracy achieves about 20% higher GDP per capita in the long run (over roughly the next 30 years)."[5] Another study suggested that the mechanism through which democracy increases GDP is by "encouraging investment, increasing schooling, inducing economic reforms, improving public good provision, and reducing social unrest."[6]

BACKGROUND

In the case of Africa, the struggle for democratization and democracy is not a new phenomenon. The genesis of the democratic movement on the continent can be traced to the colonial era when African countries were seeking independence from colonial rule. The movement eventually led to the collapse of colonialism and the beginning of the process of decolonization in the 1960s. Regrettably, the new African leaders who inherited state power from colonial rule perpetuated some of the same oppressive and exploitative policies of their colonial rulers. As Lloyd Dumas notes:

> These governments were often supported both by Cold War military rivals and outsiders determined to continue their economic domination of the newly independent nations of Africa. But they were also based on the willingness of African [leaders] to dominate and exploit other Africans. Economic development did not reach the point where the great mass of the African people experienced the tide of economic uplift that many expected or at least hoped for.[7]

Disappointed with the administration of the postcolonial state, the African peoples continued their struggle for democratization. Unfortunately, this phase of the struggle was short lived and began to lose steam by the mid-1970s. Various African authoritarian regimes responded to this movement for democracy with violence such as harassment, arrest, imprisonment, death, banishment into exile, and economic strangulation of pro-democracy activists and their supporters.

The end of the Cold War and the breakup of the Soviet Union from the late 1980s to the mid-1990s replaced the geopolitical jockeying of the superpowers with greater neglect and instability. Authoritarian regimes in Africa therefore became expendable in terms of their strategic importance to the major powers. These powers found it difficult to justify their continued support for corrupt, authoritarian, and ruthless regimes, such as Mobotu Seseko in Zaire. These regimes came to realize that as emperors, "they had on no clothes." In this environment, ethnic rivalries erupted around the continent, even to the point of tragic genocides in Rwanda and Burundi and a civil war in Liberia that led to more than a quarter-million deaths.

The democratization process that ensued was hijacked by the legacy of the past. Militarism and authoritarianism still erupt sporadically when the wave of democratic globalization was sweeping across the continent. For example, since the beginning of the twenty-first century, political uprisings have erupted in Madagascar, Tunisia, Egypt, and Libya and coups in Guinea, Mali, and Guinea-Bissau, among others.

After more than a half century of struggle and experimentation with democratic governance in Africa, democratic institutions and practices appear to be taking hold on the continent. For example, in recent years elections have led to the peaceful transfer of power in Zambia, Senegal, Ghana, and South Africa. While we have seen great progress toward a more democratic and rules-based political culture since the early 1990s, advances have become patchier, and democratic recessions have become more frequent. Recent elections in Zimbabwe, Kenya, and Côte d'Ivoire led to violence resulting in the death of many people. Coups, restriction or abolishment of constitutional term limits, and outright election rigging are recurring. Also contributing to restriction on democratic governance is the rise of China as an investor that shows no concern about good governance in the host countries.

As a result of these erratic and sporadic interferences in the process of democratization, what can be described as another wave of the democratic movement has begun. The cornerstone of this movement has been both regional and international. Some African leaders are abandoning the long-held principle of "the non-interference in the internal affairs of other countries," a principle that has perpetuated dictatorship, authoritarianism, and violation of human rights on the continent for decades. Moreover, with globalization, political instability in one country can have a significantly adverse impact on the political economies of other countries. As a result of these externalities, African leaders are now engaging in the affairs of other countries to assist in addressing political instabilities. For instance, the former president of South Africa, Thabo Mbeki, was involved in addressing the stalemate in the presidential election in neighboring Zimbabwe, which led to the migration of Zimbabwean refugees to South Africa. Some African leaders criticized the president of Zimbabwe for failing to adhere to free and fair elections for the Presidency and legislature, leading to violence and deaths. The Kenya presidential election in 2011 was characterized by violence that led to over 1000 deaths, the conventional threshold of the number of battle deaths required to constitute a civil war. The former United Nations secretary general, Kofi Anan, intervened to bring the crisis to an end. A military coup in Guinea was swiftly criticized by the Economic Community of West African States (ECOWAS) requesting for a quick transition to democratic rule. In the 2010 presidential election in Côte d'Ivoire, the defeated incumbent refused to relinquish power to the victorious opposition candidate, leading to a civil conflict. African leaders along with Western powers used military force to put the opposition candidate in power and restore stability. The incumbent was sent to The Hague, Netherlands, for war crimes. In March 2012, African leaders of ECOWAS swiftly rejected a military coup in Mali and gave an ultimatum to the military to restore the democratically elected president back to power or face isolation by member countries. The African Union also demanded a return of the country to its democratic status.

As recommended by the United Nations Economic Commission for Africa, member states should strive to promote democratic institutions and good governance in order to maintain political stability and to reduce the perceived political risks to investors.[8] Given the interdependence of the political economies of African countries, member states with politically unstable environments should be assisted to achieve stability for the benefit of the region. As noted earlier, support for the principle of the "non-interference in the internal affairs of other countries" is now eroding, creating a new impetus for the democratic struggle. African leaders and citizens, along with the international community, are now working together in promoting democratic governance on the continent, as was the case in Ivory Coast and Mali. These collaborative efforts have set a new direction for promoting democratization in Africa.

POLITICAL FREEDOM

Since 1972, Freedom House has provided annual rankings of political freedom and civil liberties for countries around the world.[9] In the case of Africa, the quest for democratic governance has been mixed. Some countries have made modest but significant gains in their quest for democratic governance, while others have not made any progress or have retrogressed. In sub-Saharan Africa (SSA), while only two countries, the Gambia and Mauritius, were considered free in 1972, eleven countries were ranked as free in 2016.[10] The countries were Benin, Botswana, Cape Verde, Ghana, Lesotho, Mali, Mauritius, Namibia, São Tomé and Príncipe, Senegal, and South Africa.[11] The number of elections per decade has also been increasing. For instance, SSA had an average of twenty-eight elections during the decades of the 1960s and 1970s. The number increased to thirty-six elections in the 1980s. During the 1990s, the number dramatically increased to sixty-five elections,[12] doubling the numbers in the 1960s and 1970s combined. As a result of the increasing trends in democratization in Africa since the 1990s,[13] Africa has experienced an increasing institutionalization of executive power and a dramatic decrease in the use of coup d'état as a means through which incumbents left office. Table 1.1 shows the various methods through which African leaders have left office and the electoral trends between 1960 and 2002.

Table 1.1 Methods of How African Leaders Left Office and the Electoral Trends (1960–2002)

Years	*1960–1989*		*1990–2002*	
Exit Mode	*Number*	*Percent*	*Number*	*Percent*
Coup, war, or invasion	79	68	25	31
Assassinated not part of a coup	2	2	2	2
Died of natural or accidental causes	9	8	3	4
Retired	8	7	14	17
Lost election	1	1	17	21
Other (interim or caretaker regime, impeachment)	18	15	20	25
Transition	117	110	81	100

Source: Daniel N. Posner and Daniel J. Young, "The Institutionalization of Political Power in Africa," *Journal of Democracy* 18, no. 3 (2007): 126–40.

While seventy-nine violent methods, such as coups d'état, war, and invasions, were used as the means of changing leadership during the period 1960–1989, only twenty-five were used during the period 1990–2002. Similarly, over the same period, the number of leaders who retired from office increased from eight to fourteen, respectively, and the number that died in office decreased from nine to three.

Albeit progress has been realized in democratic governance, the region has recently experienced some setbacks in the quest for democracy. Chad,

Madagascar, Burundi, Côte d'Ivoire, Mauritius, Somalia, Guinea, and Guinea-Bissau have experienced sharp declines. Modest declines were registered in Eritrea, Ethiopia, the Gambia, Kenya, Seychelles, and Zimbabwe.[14] For example, Congo's (Brazzaville) status declined from "partly free" to "not free" because of decrease in transparency and openness, while democratic institutions have all but collapsed in countries such as Democratic Republic of Congo (DCR), Somalia, and Sudan because of prolonged civil war. See chapter 1 for more information on the freedom rankings. Even the emerging democracy in Southern Sudan is eroding as a result of ethno-religious conflict. These factors are not only a threat to democracy but also a resurgence of authoritarian regimes.

CHALLENGE TO DEMOCRATIC CAPITALISM

As discussed earlier in this chapter, it was concluded that democratic capitalism has proven to be the best system for promoting rapid economic growth and welfare of society. This conclusion has not gone unchallenged. An issue that is frequently raised is whether the rapid expansion of the economy of the People's Republic of China, a socialist country with the second largest economy, contradicts the theory that centrally directed socialist systems do not work and cannot compete. The economic system of China, and even Russia, is different today from what it was about two decades ago when China was more socialist than it is today. The economic system has progressed more toward a free market and an open economic system. In fact it is because of China's move in the direction of a free or mixed economic system that its economic output is rapidly expanding. Similarly, the Russian economy has also expanded for the same reasons.

Tom Friedman, *New York Times* columnist, argues that when a one-party democracy is led by a reasonably enlightened group of people, as China is today, it can also have great advantages. That one party can just impose the politically difficult but critically important policies needed to move a society forward in the twenty-first century.[15]

Thus China's growth was due to an adjustment in state policy. China's imposition of critically needed policies to move its society forward may have also been influenced by globalization. This global system, which leads to internationalization of national economies, has influenced the flourishing of China's economy.

Another study has also provided an explanation for the Chines context.[16] The Communist Party has extricated itself from the socialist social contract with the urban working class without losing its grip on political power. Moreover, China has maintained a rapid pace of economic growth for more than four decades without significant political liberalization. A key factor in China's ability to reform the economy without sacrificing political control is the timing and sequencing of its foreign direct investment (FDI) liberalization. There are two key variables that are important to this comparative analysis: China's pattern of ownership diversification and China's mode of integration into the global economy. The study relates these two variables to the success of economic change without political liberalization, in particular, how FDI liberalization has affected relations between workers and the ruling Communist Party. "Reform and openness" in this context resulted in a strengthened Chinese state, a weakened civil society (especially labor), and a delay in political liberalization.

Another argument made is the case of South Africa. The apartheid system, it is argued, "generated one of the highest returns on investment of any economic system during the twentieth century, and the new democratic institutions that were developed after that country's 1994 transformation have yet to show an economic growth that could compete with the prior anti-democratic system." During the apartheid era, when development and research institutions rank countries on the level of freedom as free, partly free, or not free, South Africa was classified into two categories. When only the whites were considered, the country was classified as politically free or democratic. However, when the indigenous Africans were taken into account, the country was classified as either partly free or not free. Since the whites dominated the political and economic system, which was democratic and a free market, the economy performed well. A country can marginalize a certain group of its people and still maintain a free market system and thus a high economic prosperity. The United States, Canada, and Australia have marginalized the indigenous people in their countries as well as some blacks and yet the economies of these countries are highly developed and industrialized in the world. Because they have free market economies, despite their oppressive policies, their economies are prospering. Even though South Africa had an apartheid system, it had a free market economic system that led to its prosperity, even though this prosperity was not shared with the indigenous people.

THEME AND ORGANIZATION OF THE BOOK

The central theme of this book is to assess the status and effects of democratic governance in Africa. To this effect, the following questions will be investigated: (1) What is the African experience with democratic governance? (2) What is the status of democratic practice in Africa? (3) What is the impact of democratic governance on economic growth in Africa? What has been the role of external powers such as the United States, in promoting democratic institutions? and (4) What policies are pursued by African governments to promote democratic governance on the continent? The assessment of democratic governance in Africa will consist of continental and sub-regional approaches. The sub-regions are:

- West Africa
- North Africa
- East Africa
- Southern Africa
- Central Africa

The rest of this book is organized as follows. In chapter 2, political economy is presented as the theoretical foundation employed in the discussion of democratic governance. Chapter 3 presents the trends in democratic governance in each sub-region since the beginning of independence on the continent. The political economy concepts defined in chapter 2 are applied to sub-regional analysis.

In the next two chapters we provide case studies of countries in which we assess the relationship among democracy, governance, and economic growth. In chapter 4 we compare the performance of democratic institutions in South Africa and Ghana. These two countries have received international recognition as countries in which democratic governance flourished decades ago. In chapter 5, we assess the impact of democratic governance in the case of Nigeria. The country was selected because of its unique background or characteristics as the country with the largest population and the most number of coups d'état on the continent. As a result, the country has had a very turbulent political economic history.

During the presidency of William Jefferson Clinton of the United States, the African Growth and Opportunity Act was enacted, whereby the United States would promote trade with African countries that promote political reforms and democratic market institutions. The act authorizes the president to designate countries as eligible to receive the benefits of African Growth and Opportunity Act (AGOA) if the countries are determined to have established or are making continual progress toward establishing the following: "market-based economies; the rule of law and political pluralism; elimination of barriers to US trade and investment; protection of intellectual property; efforts to combat corruption; policies to reduce poverty, increasing availability of health care and educational opportunities; protection of human rights and worker rights; and elimination of certain child labor practices."[17] In chapter 6, we assess the impact of AGOA on trade and democratic institutions on the continent.

Chapter 7, the closing chapter, discusses the response of African leaders to the need for democratic governance. The response is derived from the assessment of the various African governmental organizations since independence. The chapter examines the major contours of each of these institutions and assesses their impact. The trends in the formation of these institutions indicate that African leaders have realized from their experiences that peace, security, democracy, good governance, human rights, and sound economic management are essential for sustainable development. They have therefore pledged to work, both individually and collectively, to promote these principles in their countries, sub-regions and the continent in a document known as the New Partnership for Africa's Development (NEPAD). The effectiveness and challenges of NEPAD as instrument for promoting democratic governance on the continent are assessed.

NOTES

1. Adam Smith, *An inquiry into the Nature and Causes of the Wealth of Nations* (London: Methuen & Company, 1776).
2. Jamil Jreisat, *Globalism and Comparative Public Administration* (New York: CRC Press, 2012), 15–16.
3. Brian J. L. Berry, Edgar C. Conkling, and D. Michael Ray, *The Global Economy: Resource Use, Locational Choice, and International Trade* (Englewood Cliffs, NJ: Prentice Hall, 1993), 2.
4. Thomas Plumper and Christian W Martin, "Democracy, Government Spending, and Economic Growth: A Political-Economic Explanation of the Barro-Effect," *Public Choice* 117, nos. 1–2 (2003).
5. Daron Acemoglu, Suresh Naidu, James Robinson, and Pascual Restrepo, "Democracy Causes Economic Development?" *VOX CEPR Policy Portal* (May 19, 2014). http://voxeu.org/article/democracy-and-growth-new-evidence. Retrieved November 23, 2016.
6. Daron Acemoglu, Suresh Naidu, Pascual Restrepo, and James A. Robinson, " Democracy Does Cause Growth," *NBER Working Paper*, No. 2004 (Issued in March 2014): NBER Program(s): DEV EFG POL.
7. Lloyd Dumas, "Democratization and Demilitarization: Building Peace and Prosperity in Africa," *Developmental Policy Studies*: *The Newsletter-Journal of the National PSO's* 5, no. 1 (Spring 1999), 13.
8. United Nations Economic Commission for Africa (UNECA), *Harmonization of Mining Policies, Standards, Legislative and Regulatory Frameworks in Southern Africa* (Southern Africa Office: UNECA, 2004), 17.
9. Freedom House. *"Freedom in the World: Country Ratings 1972–2005."* http://www.FreedomHouse.org.
10. Freedom House, *"Freedom in the World: Country Ratings 1972–2005."* See also Arch Puddington *"Freedom in the World 2007: Freedom Stagnation Amid Pushback against Democracy."* http://www.freedomhouse.org.

11. Freedom House, "*Freedom in the World: Country Ratings 1972–2005*."
12. Ibid.
13. Daniel N. Posner and Daniel J. Young, "The Institutionalization of Political Power in Africa," *Journal of Democracy* 18, no. 3 (July 2007), 130.
14. Ibid.
15. Acemoglu, Naidu, Robinson, and Restrepo, "Democracy Causes Economic Development?"; World Economic Forum, *Agenda: The Stories shaping the Global, Regional and Industry Agendas 2014*. https://www.weforum.org/agenda. Acemoglu, Naidu, Restrepo, and Robinson, "Democracy Does Cause Growth."
16. Mary E. Gallagher, "Reform and Openness: Why China's Economic Reforms Have Delayed Democracy," *World Politics* 54, no. 3 (April 2002), 338. DOI: https://doi.org/10.1353/wp.2002.0009. https://www.cambridge.org/core/journals/world-politics/article/reform-and-openness-why-chinas-economic-reforms-have-delayed-democracy/F04522C8CB83590B9B819486782BAB7E.
17. "African Growth and Opportunity Act," http://www.agoa.gov/eligibility/country_eligibility.html.

Chapter 2

Concepts of Democratic Governance

A political economy framework is employed in the analysis of democratic governance in Africa. Political economy has a variety of definitions which can determine how it is applied in policy analysis. One definition refers to political economy as the study of the political basis of economic actions, that is, the ways in which government policies affect market operations. Another definition refers to political economy as the study of the economic basis of political action, that is, the ways in which economic forces influence government policies. These two definitions are complementary, since politics and markets are in a constant state of mutual interaction. These two perspectives of political economy are employed in this study. The key political economy variables that are employed in this study include governance, good governance, democracy, political freedom, and the size of government.

GOVERNANCE

Although the concept of governance is not new in policy circles,[1] in recent years, the terms "governance" and "good governance" have increasingly received a renewed interest in the development literature and in political and policy circles. The term "governance" has been defined in various ways by various world leaders and development institutions. For example, according to the former Secretary General of the United Nations, Kofi Anan, "good governance is ensuring respect for human rights and the rule of law; strengthening democracy; promoting transparency and capacity in public administration."[2] The World Bank defines[3] governance as the manner in which power is exercised in the management of a country's economic and social resources. The World Bank has identified the following three distinct aspects of governance: (1) the form of political regime; (2) the process by which authority is exercised in the management of a country's economic and social resources for development; and (3) the capacity of governments to design, formulate, and implement policies and discharge function (World Bank, 1997). The United Nations Development Programme (UNDP) also views governance as the exercise of economic, political, and administrative authority to manage a country's affairs at all levels. It comprises mechanisms, processes, and institutions through which citizens and groups articulate their interests, exercise their legal rights, meet their obligations, and mediate their differences (UNDP, 1997). Last, but not the least, according to the Organization of Economic Cooperation and Development (OECD), the concept of governance denotes the use of political authority and exercise of control in a society in relation to the management of its resources for social and economic development. This broad definition encompasses the role of public authorities in establishing the environment in which economic operators function and in determining the distribution of benefits as well as the nature of the relationship between the ruler and the ruled (OECD DAC, 1995).

GOOD GOVERNANCE

The concept of good governance is relatively new. In its 1989 report, the World Bank referred to the crisis in the SSA region as a "crisis of governance."[4] The main thrust behind its introduction in the Bank's corporate policies resides in "the continuing lack of the effectiveness of aid, the feeble commitment to reform in recipient governments, and the persistence of endemic corruption in developing countries."[5] The Bank's founding charter prohibits it from taking political considerations into account when designing developmental assistance. However, with the increasing linkage between political and economic globalization, the Bank has come to realize that the quality of a country's governance system is a key determinant of the ability to pursue sustainable economic and social development. Thus, empirical studies of the political economy of policy reform suggest that the influence of political context on economic performance is important. For example, studies have found that economies of countries with political freedom or democratic institutions grow at a faster rate than economies of countries in which these freedoms or institutions are proscribed.[6] Another study went as far as suggesting that a country that switches from non-democracy to democracy achieves about 20 percent higher GDP per capita over the subsequent three decades.[7] The need for a political economy approach in assessing governance, democracy, and development is clearly evident.

Good governance is participatory, consensus-oriented, accountable, transparent, responsive, effective and efficient, and equitable and inclusive, and follows the rule of law. It assures that corruption is minimized, the views of minorities are taken into account, and the voices of the most vulnerable in society are heard in decision making. It is also responsive to the present and future needs of the society.

Other studies also have provided six dimensions of good governance consisting of:[8]

1. voice and accountability, which includes civil liberties and political stability;
2. government effectiveness, which includes the quality of policymaking and public service delivery;
3. the lack of regulatory burden;
4. the rule of law, which includes protection of property rights;
5. independence of the judiciary; and
6. control of corruption.

Using aggregate governance indicators corresponding to these six dimensions of governance, these studies found a strong positive causal relationship from governance to better development outcomes.[9] Thus, good governance is essential for development.

Governance, democracy, and economic growth are also interlinked. Although theoretically good governance and democracy may be promoted independently from each other, they often overlap in practice. Good governance requires an efficient executive, a functioning legislature, an independent judiciary, and the effective balance and separation of powers, all of which are constituent elements of a democratic regime. As a result, good governance is not sustainable without effective democratic institutions, and both are essential for successful development. Empirical evidence on the impact of governance and democracy on economic growth in Africa are provided in subsequent chapters.

DEMOCRACY AND POLITICAL FREEDOM

Democracy implies the right of all adults to vote and compete for public office to elect representatives and have decisive vote on public policies that truly reflect the interests and opinions of the citizens. The holding of elections is only one aspect of democracy. It also means the right to free expression; the free flow of information in the society so that citizens can be well informed about public policy issues and effective participation in government to form civil society organizations; organize or demonstrate; and freedom of religion, education, travel, and other personal rights.

Combining democracy and governance provides the political economy variable that encapsulates the two factors as democratic governance, which is measured using two indices—the Freedom House indices of political freedom and the Ibrahim Index of African Governance (IIAG). Since 1972, Freedom House has published annual country rankings of political and civil liberties, types of economic systems, and other measures of freedom. Freedom rankings are derived from political rights and civil liberties. Political rights are rights to participate meaningfully in the political process. In a democracy, this means the right of all adults to vote and compete for public office and for elected representatives to have a decisive vote on public policies. Civil Liberties are rights to free expression, to organize or demonstrate, and freedom of religion, education, travel, and other personal rights. Freedom House rates political rights and civil liberties on a 7–point scale, with 7 being the least free or least democratic and 1 being the most free or most democratic. From this scale, Freedom House derives the annual status of political freedom for each country, with 1 to 2.5 classified as free or democratic, 3 to 5 classified as partly free or partly democratic, and 5.5 to 7 as not free or not democratic. The degree of political freedom is adapted from these Freedom House's country rankings[10] and are applied individually to various countries, as well as sub-regions consisting of West Africa, East Africa, North Africa, Central Africa, and Southern Africa over the years.

The other measure of governance is the IIAG, with its publication beginning in 2007. The IIAG was created to provide a quantifiable tool to measure and monitor governance in African countries and assess it progress over time in order to support the development of effective responsive policy solutions. For this purpose, the IIAG defined governance as the provision of the political, social, and economic public goods and services that every citizen has the right to expect from the state and that a state has the responsibility to deliver to its citizens. The Overall Governance Index is derived from the combination of four categories of indicators namely Safety and Rule of Law, Participation and Human Rights, Sustainable Economic Opportunity, and Human Development. The four categories are subdivided into fourteen subcategories which are derived from ninety-five indicators. In total, there were 237 measures of governance in Africa in the 2016 IIAG. This construction method provides the most comprehensive amount of robust data on African governance. The recent index, reported in 2016, focused on analyzing the past decade of governance from 2006 to 2015. The index is applied to fifty-four African countries, with sixteen years' worth of data from 2000 to 2015 inclusive. Countries are placed in five groups based on their scores for overall governance:

1. High	71.0 and above
2. Medium-high	54.0–70.9
3. Medium	41.0–53.9
4. Medium-low	23.0–40.9
5. Low	Below 23.0

The two extremes are the highest band in overall governance with a score equal to or above 71 points, representing the best performance on the continent, while the lowest band is a score below 23 points representing the lowest performance on the continent. Medium-high, medium, and medium-low performance fall between the two extremes.

Government Size

Another political economy variable is the size of government measured as the share of government expenditure in GDP. The data are derived from several international sources such as the United Nations, the World Bank, and the United Nations Economic Commission for Africa.

SUMMARY

Democratic governance in Africa is assessed from both regional and continental perspectives. To this effect, a political economy framework is employed. Concepts employed are defined and provide a framework and foundation for assessing democratic governance in Africa. These concepts include democracy, good governance, openness of the economy, and the size of government.

NOTES

1. http://www.unescap.org/pdd/prs/ProjectActivities/Ongoing/gg/governance.asp. Retrieved May 28, 2012.
2. http://www.unescap.org/pdd/prs/ProjectActivities/Ongoing/gg/governance.asp.
3. Thomas G Weiss, "Governance, Good Governance and Global Governance: Conceptual and Actual Challenges," *Third World Quarterly* 21, no. 5 (2000). United Nations Development Programme (UNDP), *Governance for Sustainable Human Development: A UNDP Policy Document.* http://mirror.undp.org/magnet/policy/chapter1.htm.

4. Carlos Santiso, "Good Governance and Aid Effectiveness: The World Bank and Conditionality," *The Georgetown Public Policy Review* 7, no. 1 (Fall 2001), 3.

5. Santiso, "Good Governance and Aid Effectiveness."

6. James S. Guseh, "Government Size and Economic Growth in Developing Countries: A Political-Economy Framework," *Journal of Macroeconomics* 19, no. 1 (Winter 1997), 181.

7. Daron Acemoglu, Suresh Naidu, James Robinson, and Pascual Restrepo, May 19, 2014 "Democracy causes economic development?" http://voxeu.org/article/democracy-and-growth-new-evidence.

8. Kaufmann, Kraay, and Zoido-Lobatón, "Governance Matters," World Bank Policy Research Working Paper No. 2196 (Washington, DC, 1999). www.worldbank.org/wbi/governance/. Retrieved April 15, 2014.

9. Kaufmann, Kraay, and Zoido-Lobatón, "Governance Matters."

10. Freedom House, "Freedom in the World." http://www.freedomhouse.org. Retrieved April 12, 2014.

Chapter 3

Democratic Governance in Africa

Trends and Assessment

Since the 1960s and 1970s when most SSA countries gained independence from colonial rule, achieving freedom, economic growth, and development has been a central objective of governments in the region, as well as international donor organizations. The Organization of African Unity, now the African Union, was established to promote, among other things, the integration of African economies and their development at the economic, social, and cultural levels.[1]

African regional organizations, such as the ECOWAS, East African Community, and Southern African Development Community, were established to promote economic development in their respective sub-regions. At the same time, there are many international development institutions, such as the United Nations, African Development Bank, World Bank, and the International Monetary Fund that have been involved in the development of Africa and other developing regions. These institutions, as well as governments of many developed countries, have also provided substantial development assistance. Despite the numerous institutions and substantial resources devoted to the development of SSA, success has been scattered and slow. As stated above, countries with democratic institutions tend to realize better economic performance. Accordingly, in the next section, we provide an in-depth analysis of democratic governance and trends in each of the sub-regions in Africa: West Africa, East Africa, Central Africa, and Southern Africa. This will also facilitate a comparative analysis of democratic governance in the sub-regions including their successes and challenges.

WEST AFRICA

The West African sub-region comprises sixteen countries: Benin, Burkina Faso, Cape Verde, Côte d'Ivoire, Gambia, Ghana, Guinea, Guinea-Bissau,

Liberia, Mali, Mauritania, Niger, Nigeria, Senegal, Sierra Leone, and Togo. Two of these countries, Liberia and Ghana, have very long histories of independence, not only in the sub-region, but also in the African continent. Liberia, which was never colonized, is the oldest independent country in Africa, and except for Sudan, Ghana is the first country in the sub-region to gain independence from colonial rule.

Democratic governance in the sub-region has been progressing, although with some setbacks. In 1972, the first year in which Freedom House, the international nongovernmental organization, published annual country rankings of the level of freedom or democracy, only one country in the sub-region, Gambia, was ranked free, and ten were ranked as not free. Since then the number of countries ranked free increased to three in 1980, but declined to one in 1990. Since 1972 the number of countries ranked free more than tripled by 2011, while the number of not free countries declined from ten to two over the same period. The 1990s was a turbulent period in democratic governance when there were some setbacks. As table 3.1 shows, the number of countries ranked free declined from three in 1980 to one in 1990. This may be attributed to civil wars in Liberia, Sierra Leone, Côte d'Ivoire, and other countries during the 1990s and early 2000s. Although the trends indicate that democratic governance is gradually taking hold in West Africa, much still needs to be realized, especially when 75 percent of the countries are not democratic.

In 1975, countries in West Africa formed an organization called the ECOWAS with the goal of economic cooperation and integration of its member states to promote economic growth and development. Presently, ECOWAS has fifteen members, since Mauritania left the organization. The founding charter of the organization aimed at achieving unity and development, but did not address political, peace, and security issues. The lack of such policy would later lead to a policy lag in the formulation and implementation of policies to address conflicts that would threaten peace and democratization in the sub-region. Policy lag inhibits the ability of public organizations to respond to situations in their policy environments by letting the responses of the implementing organizations lag behind the need for the response.[2] With no established policy to address civil war and inter-state conflict in the sub-region, the leaders in the sub-region could not easily come to one accord on what to do.

About three years after the adoption of the charter, ECOWAS faced inter-state problems with which it had no legal authority to intervene. To address this state of flux, ECOWAS adopted two protocols. The 1978 Protocol on Non-Aggression stated that in the case of disagreements between states, they would commit to resolving their differences through peaceful means and dialog. The 1995 Protocol on Mutual Assistance stated that if a state is aggressed, the other states will come to its defense.

Table 3.1 Democratic Trends in West African Countries for Selected Years

Status of Freedom	*1972*	*1980*	*1990*	*2000*	*2011*	*2015*
Free	1	3	1	3	4	3
Partly free	3	5	6	10	10	10
Not free	10	8	9	3	2	3
Total	14	16	16	16	16	16

Note: Data not available for Cape Verde and Guinea-Bissau for 1972 resulting in a total of fourteen countries.
Source: Compiled from Freedom House (2018).

Shortly after the adoptions, intra-state conflicts arose in Liberia, followed by similar conflicts in Sierra Leone, Côte d'Ivoire, Guinea, and other countries. Since the protocols dealt with inter-state conflicts, they could not apply to the Liberian Civil War. ECOWAS therefore came up with an *ad hoc* solution through its Mediation Committee to deal with the Liberian conflict by deploying a monitoring force commonly known as ECOMOG, Economic Community Monitoring Group, to bring about and monitor a cease-fire. Recently, military coups have erupted in Mali and Guinea-Bissau which ECOWAS is dealing with through threat or use of sanctions, military force, and expulsion from the association.

Thus, the formulation and implementation of ECOWAS' policies in addressing its sub-regional security issues has tended to lag behind the immediate need for the response. ECOWAS approach has tended to be more reactive than proactive. What is needed is for ECOWAS to build a certain degree of automaticity into the policy response or at least to provide some insulation against any political delay or interference.

Related to the problem of policy lag is the problem of inadequate consideration of the underlying theory of causation. The process of effective policy implementation depends to a large extent on, among other factors, knowledge of the pattern of causation and information about the policy area. In the West Africa sub-region, there are several indicators of threat to security, such as coups d'état, civil wars, and inter-state conflicts. If the underlying process of causation of these indicators is misunderstood or not understood, there is little hope of effectively implementing a policy choice. For instance, the ECOWAS leaders, as well as Liberian citizens, have not understood the underlying cause of the Liberian Civil War. Thus, the eruption of any of these indicators, such as the civil wars in Liberia and coup d'état in Guinea-Bissau, may trigger relatively standard reactions, such as sanctions, expulsion, and/or military intervention. In these situations, the policymakers often wind up treating the symptoms instead of the underlying causal process. Despite ECOWAS interventions in conflicts in the sub-region, through the use of threat of sanctions, expulsions, and military intervention, the region continues to experience sporadic eruptions of conflicts that are hampering the process of democratization that was emerging not only in the sub-region, but also in the rest of the continent.

Except for the Great Lakes region with the genocide in Rwanda, the democratization process has been more turbulent in West Africa than any other sub-region on the continent. The democratization process has been unfurling against the background of military coups and a civil war, which have had a devastating effect on the standard of living in those countries.

All countries in the sub-region have had military or a one-party rule at some point in time, thereby obstructing the pursuit of democracy. For example, Guinea, which gained independence from France in 1958, was under a nondemocratic rule until 2010 when it had its first democratic election. Its first head of state at the time of independence, Seko Toure, governed under a one-party system for twenty-six consecutive years. After his death in 1982, the military succeeded him and ruled under a one-party system for twenty-four years till 2008 when the first democratically free election was held. Similarly, Guinea-Bissau, which gained independence from Portugal 1974, had been governed mostly under military rule. In 2009 the military handed power to a democratically elected government for five years. Another example is Mauritania, which gained independence in 1960, held its first democratic election in 2007 followed the next year (2008) by a military coup. The military leader won the election in 2009 for a five-year term.

In fact, over the last twenty years, this sub-region has witnessed the longest and bloodiest conflicts. West Africa is going through a tumultuous democratic process whose continuity is itself under constant threat. As one writer put it "West Africa may be compared to a volcanic area with blowouts here and there and other hotspots waiting to erupt." In all, West Africa is witnessing a period of particularly difficult democratic transition. Until ECOWAS can begin to address the underlying cause of the conflicts and their attendant erosion of democracy, the sub-region will continue to face challenges in its quest for democracy, democratization, and sustainable development. The Ebola crises that began in the sub-region in 2014 have exacerbated the challenge to achieving sustainable development.

EAST AFRICA

The countries that comprise the East African sub-region depend on which institution is providing the information. For the purpose of this book, the list of countries employed is provided by the United Nations Economic Commission for Africa. The countries in the East African sub-region are listed in table 3.2 along with their rankings of freedom. In addition to

Table 3.2 Freedom Rankings in East African Countries for Selected Years

No	*Country*	*1975*	*1985*	*1995*	*2005*	*2015*
1	Burundi	N	N	N	P	N
2	Comoros	P	N	P	P	P
3	D.R. Congo	N	N	N	N	N
4	Djibouti	–	N	N	P	N
5	Ethiopia	N	N	P	P	N
6	Eritrea	–	–	P	N	N
7	Kenya	P	P	N	P	P
8	Madagascar	P	P	P	P	P
9	Rwanda	N	N	N	N	N
10	Seychelles	–	N	P	P	P
11	Somalia	N	N	N	N	N
12	South Sudan	–	–		–	N
13	Tanzania	N	N	P	P	P
14	Uganda	N	P	P	P	N

Note: F = free; PF = partly free; NF = not free.
Source: Compiled from Freedom House (2016). The East African Region. http://exploringafrica.matrix.msu.edu/students/curriculum/m19/activity1.php.

having been colonized, the countries have been mired by political instability, authoritarianism, violent conflicts, and corruption as indicated by the low freedom rankings shown in table 3.3. Among the three categories used to rank countries based on the level of freedom, none of the countries achieved the highest freedom ranking—they were either ranked partly free or not free.

Examples of countries clearly attest to this status of freedom. In Ethiopia, the government increasingly used its antiterrorism legislation to repress political opponents[3] as indicated in its low freedom ranking. In Kenya, two men ruled the country in succession with iron hands from independence in 1963 to 2002. Jomo Kenyatta ruled from 1963 to 1978; Daniel Arap Moi from 1978 to 2002. In addition to the harsh political environment, the country was also beset by corruption. In the 2002 national election, a new political party defeated the incumbent party that had ruled the country since independence. The new party however failed to fulfill promises of accountability and avoided appointments of members of his ethnic group in government. As a

Table 3.3 Democratic Trends in East Africa Countries for Selected Years

Category of Freedom	*1975*	*1985*	*1990*	*1995*	*2015*
Free	0	0	0	0	0
Partly free	3	3	7	9	5
Not free	7	9	6	4	9
Total	10	12	13	13	14

Source: Compiled from Freedom House (2016). The East African Region. http://exploringafrica.matrix.msu.edu/students/curriculum/m19/activity1.php.

result the frustration of the people led to the violence that took place after the election in 2007, thereby impeding the democratic progress.

Another country, Burundi, went through twelve years of ethnic violence that sparked off in 1994 between its usually dominant Tutsi minority and the Hutu majority. The war led to the deaths of 200,000 people and the internal and external displacement of hundreds of thousands of Burundians. In 2015 the country was plunged into turmoil when the incumbent president decided to run for a third controversial term. Burundi's constitution did provide that a president can only serve for two terms. However, the incumbent president claimed that he was eligible for another term, because he was elected by lawmakers and not by the people for what was being considered his first term. Since his election was not by the people, it did not count as a term. In the end, he won the election for the controversial term. Great Britain, the United States, and the United Nations condemned the election as not been free and fair, because of harassment and intimidation of the opposition, civil rights activists, journalists, and voters.

Rwanda is known for its horrific civil war between the majority Hutu ethnic group and the minority Tutsis ethnic group in 1994. The war resulted in a genocide with an estimated one million Rwandans killed. Rwandan President Paul Kagame is not just a dictator responsible for human rights abuses, but he has great many friends. He is credited for commanding the rebel force that ended the genocide. Since then he has been the defacto leader of Rwanda. Many world leaders, such as Bill Clinton of the United States, Tony Blair of Great Britain, and the UN Secretary General Ban Ki-moon have commended him for good leadership. Leaders of other countries, such as Netherlands and Germany, have joined the bandwagon of praises. It is also reported that Washington has also shielded Kagame from the International Criminal Tribunal for Rwanda (ICTR), set up to prosecute killings during the genocide.[4]

Kagame, however, has detractors. Although the country is stable given that it had come from an era of genocide, the government has some detractors criticizing him for human rights violation and political oppression. According to Human Rights Watch and Amnesty International, in recent years perhaps half a dozen well-known investigators, journalists, and opposition politicians have been found dead in mysterious circumstances, including a Rwandan Transparency International worker who had been investigating police corruption.

No country is ranked in the political free category. The number of countries in the not free category has been fluctuating over the years. The number of politically free countries peaked to nine countries in 1985 and declined to its lowest of four countries in 1995. In 2015, it again peaked to nine countries. These results indicated the political volatility of the region. The region needs commitment to political freedom to achieve peace and stability.

NORTH AFRICA

North African states experienced greater openness in areas such as freedom of press prior to 2006, primarily as a result of the Pan Arab satellite television networks such as Al Jazeera, and greater access to worldwide information through the Internet.[5] This openness, however, was not accompanied by good governance. According to Jamil Jreisat, accumulation of incremental adjustments that results in gradual institutional transformation assumes an open and representative government with legitimate leadership that enjoys public trust and confidence in its competence and integrity.[6]

During the early days of 2011, the world witnessed a forceful demand for reform in the Arab world. The popular uprisings were against autocratic leaders, rampant corruption, institutional weakness, and inept public leaders and managers who were mainly employed and appointed through nepotism and favoritism. Moreover, lack of freedom and economic opportunity pushed previously silent and frustrated young people to press forward for a radical change of regime. Political freedom was restrained considerably in most of North Africa until 2011 when mass protests in some of the countries led to the removal of their heads of state in their quest for political freedom. Table 3.4 shows the trends in democratic governance in North Africa from 1972 to 2011.

These uprisings, referred to as the Arab Spring, swept across North Africa and the Middle East beginning with mass protests and demonstrations. The massive public protests and acts of discontent in the North African and Arab countries forced political leaders out of office in some countries and threatened others with a similar destiny unless the system of governance was fundamentally reformed. This wave began in Tunisia when a young street vendor set himself ablaze in protest of police harassment and brutality in December 2010. This act led to a mass protest against President Ben Ali of Tunisia, resulting in his fleeing to Saudi Arabia in January 2011. The Tunisian uprising had a domino effect in the sub-region. It was followed by another mass protest in Egypt leading to the resignation of the president, Hoseni Mubarak,

Table 3.4 Democratic Trends in North African Countries for Selected Years

Status of Freedom	*1972*	*1980*	*1990*	*2000*	*2010*	*2015*
Free	0	0	0	0	0	1
Partially free	1	4	4	1	1	1
Not free	5	2	2	5	5	4
Total	6	6	6	6	6	6

Source. Compiled from Freedom House (2015). United Nations Economic Commission for Africa. https://www.uneca.org/sro-na.

ending his thirty-year rule. Subsequently, the military assumed power promising to hold elections in 2012. A two-day election for president was held on May 2 and 26 of that year and the leader of the military coup was declared the winner.

The next country was Libya, where the democratic struggle began in February 2011 with protests that erupted into an armed conflict. With the assistance of NATO, including the training of Libyan opposition forces and control of the Libyan airspace through a no-fly zone, the president, Mohammed Gadhafi, was overthrown in August 2011 and assassinated in October of the same year. Since then the country has been beset by political instability with no clear leader in place. These quests for reform in the Arab world also spread to Yemen, Bahrain, and the rest of the Arab world. Regardless of the wishes of the outside world, the Arab people provided the determination to change the history of their countries from within.

Algeria was the only country in North Africa that was not impacted by the Arab Spring. Algeria has experienced a turbulent political history since its independence from France in 1962 until the 1990s. However, between 2004 and 2007 the government of President Abdul-Aziz Boutefiika took measures to reduce political conflict and violence among factional and religious groups within the state. Thus, the Boutefiika administration instituted a "National Reconciliation Policy" in 2005 that laid out principles for reconciliation and amnesty for insurgent groups.[7] In light of the reconciliation efforts, the Boutefiika administration was faced with the challenges of democratic and market reforms.[8]

In 2009, the Boutefiika administration won a third-term election after the government amended the constitution in 2008 to remove presidential term limits.[9]

SURGE IN REFUGEES CROSSING THE MEDITERRANEAN SEA

The state of flux following the civil war and the assassination of its president has created a lax environment that has made it easier for smugglers to transport war victims through the country to Europe.[10] As a result, the number of refugees fleeing war and poverty in the Middle East, Northeastern Africa, Afghanistan, and other parts of Africa to reach Europe via the Mediterranean Sea has surged since 2014. Desperately seeking a place of refuge, more than 1800 migrants may have drowned from rickety boats and unsafe ships by mid-2015 in their attempts to travel to Europe. Many of the refugees begin their journey in the backs of trucks, which smugglers use to transport them through the desert into Libya.

Many refugees sought asylum in countries like Italy, Germany, and Sweden. As the refugee surge continues, the debate is growing in the European Union about the lack of unified immigration policies and funding for migrant rescue operations. The surge is also threating the promotion of democratic governance in the Arab world.

SOUTHERN AFRICA

Democratic institutions in Southern Africa is an evolving pursuit that has not easily taken root in light of the demise of the white settler system of apartheid, beginning with Zimbabwe in 1980 and South Africa in 1994. However, the region is relatively peaceful except for authoritarian rule in Zimbabwe. Moreover, social discontent in South Africa sparked by high unemployment spurred violence through xenophobia and regional security issues among member states of the Southern African Community (SADC).[11] As a result, South Africa has experienced an overall decline in the area of governance from high to medium-high. In fact, South Africa is one of the six countries that have shown deterioration in overall governance that has led to a downward movement in the governance barometer band.[12] Despite this development, the region is relatively peaceful, and democratic rule is slowly taking hold as indicated in table 3.5.

However, the consolidation of democracy has slowly evolved in countries such as Zimbabwe, Angola and Swaziland in the last decade. For instance, by the 2002 elections, Zimbabwe experienced a shift in electoral participation and contestation. The perennial one-party system that had been almost a permanent political feature was challenged by the Movement of Democratic Change (MDC). Thus, political participation began to take on a different character. In response, the Mugabe administration employed various forms of political and judicial intimidation to deter opposition groups. It is along this line that one can better understand the land reform policy instituted by the Mugabe administration.

The administration had evicted 90 percent of white commercial farmers from an estimated 10.5 million hectares of farmlands in anticipation of

Table 3.5 Democratic Trends in Southern Africa for Selected Years

Status of Freedom	*1975*	*1985*	*1995*	*2005*	*2015*
Free	2	2	5	5	5
Partially free	4	5	4	3	3
Not free	5	3	2	3	3
Total	11	10	11	11	11

Source: Compiled from Freedom House Sub-Saharan Africa. https://freedomhouse.org/regions/sub-saharan-africa. Retrieved September 11, 2016.

redistributing the land to indigenous Zimbabweans.[13] It was estimated that the administration had redistributed land to 110,000 households, in some cases for political support. This was the case during the elections of 2002. In other cases, cabinet members and party stalwarts benefited from the land redistribution program.[14]

The failure of the land redistribution program and the attendant economic crisis that the country encountered polarized the electorate. It is against this background that the Zimbabwe African National Union (ZANU) experienced a defeat in the 2008 elections. The party lost its majority seat in the lower House of Assembly by two after twenty-eight years of dominance through authoritarian control. Along the same line, the 2008 elections produced an electoral deadlock in which none of the four presidential candidates—Robert Mugabe, Morgan Tsvangirai, Simba Makoni, and Langton Towungana—received a majority.[15] The outcome of this political deadlock was a runoff election between Robert Mugabe (ZANU-PF) and Morgan Tsvangirai (MDC). The runoff, which was scheduled for June 2008, produced a run-away victory for Mugabe. Tsvangirai withdrew from the process because several MDC supporters were killed and intimidated by government authorities.[16] Nonetheless, Mugabe was promptly sworn in as the president-elect two days after the runoff. Given the intense opposition to the outcome of the runoff from civil society in Zimbabwe and the international community, the Mugabe administration, Tsvanigrai, and other opposition groups agreed to a power-sharing coalition government in February 2009. Mugabe remained president and Tsvangirai became the prime minister. Zimbabwe has been mired by political turmoil under the leadership of President Robert Mugabe. The political unrest in Zimbabwe is primarily driven by interparty and intraparty rivalry with the ruling party ZANU-PF and the major opposition party MDC.[17]

However, recent democratic trends in SSA show that Zimbabwe has begun to experience progress in the four categories of democratic measurements—"human rights, rule of law, sustainable economic opportunity, and human development" in the last decade. This improvement has pushed Zimbabwe out of the bottom ten countries in overall governance to the thirty ninth rank in 2015.[18] The improvement is attributed to progress in the area of sustainable economic opportunity which has peaked beyond other sub-categories. In addition, Zimbabwe has registered the largest improvement in public management and rural sector on the continent.[19]

By 2015 the Southern African region had remained the highest scoring region in the overall governance category. The region comprises the top ten scoring countries in SSA. It is also considered the best performing region with the highest average regional score of 58.3 points in 2015.[20] The region has demonstrated improvement in all categories except in safety and the rule of law, where it has shown a deterioration of 1.6 points. Along the same lines,

Table 3.6 Freedom Rankings in the Central African Region for Selected Years

Countries	*1975*	*1985*	*1995*	*2005*	*2015*
Cameroon	PF	NF	NF	NF	NF
Chad	NF	NF	NF	NF	NF
Central African Republic	NF	NF	PF	NF	NF
Congo-Brazzaville	PF	NF	PF	PF	NF
Equatorial Guinea	NF	NF	NF	NF	NF
Gabon	NF	NF	PF	PF	NF
São Tomé Príncipe	PF	NF	F	F	F

Note: F = free; NF = not free; PF = partially free.
Source: Compiled from Freedom House Sub-Saharan Africa Report. https://freedomhouse.org/regions/sub-saharan-africa. Retrieved September 11, 2016.

accountability has also declined in Southern Africa by 4.0 points since 2006; this is the main reason for the decline in the score for safety and the rule of law.[21]

CENTRAL AFRICAN REGION

The Central African region comprises seven countries with the Democratic Republic of the Congo (Kinshasa) being the largest country. Gabon is included along with the Central African Republic because of their common historical ties. Both of these countries were once part of the French Equatorial Africa. Rwanda and Burundi, although they are located east of the East African Rift System, which forms the eastern divide of the Congo basin, are also often considered part of the region because of their long administrative connections with the former Belgian Congo, now Congo Kinshasa. The island republic of São Tomé and Príncipe, off the Atlantic coast of Gabon, is also included in the region.[22]

Besides São Tomé and Príncipe, most of the countries in the Central African region have been either partly free or not free from 1975 to 2015.[23] To further accentuate the political volatility in the region, tables 3.6 and 3.7 below show the freedom rankings of the countries in the region and a summary of these rankings for the region, respectively. The political briefs of

Table 3.7 Total of Freedom Rankings in the Central African Region for Selected Years

Status of Freedom	*1975*	*1985*	*1995*	*2005*	*2015*
Free	0	0	1	1	1
Partially free	3	0	3	2	0
Not free	4	7	3	4	6
Total	7	7	7	7	7

Source: Compiled from Freedom House Sub-Saharan Africa Report. https://freedomhouse.org/regions/sub-saharan-africa. Retrieved September 11, 2016.

Central African Republic and Cameroon below provide a parallel reflection of the democratic trends in the region.

The Central African Republic

The Central African Republic was a former French colony until the attainment of independence in 1960 and David Dacko became the first president of the country. The country has enjoyed little peace or stability since gaining its independence. On January 1, 1966, following an almost bloodless coup, Colonel Jean-Bedel Bokassa forcefully assumed power. He abolished the constitution of 1959, dissolved the National Assembly, and issued a decree that placed all legislative and executive powers in the hands of the president. On December 4, 1976, the republic became a monarchy with the promulgation of the imperial constitution and the proclamation of the president as Emperor Bokassa I. His regime suffered from numerous human rights atrocities.[24] For example, as many as one hundred children were murdered because they had resisted wearing his government-produced school uniforms. He was an ally of France, the murder of the school children became too much for his French ally. On September 20, 1979, the former president, David Dacko, led a successful French-backed coup against Bokassa, ending the emperor's brutal reign.

Dacko's efforts to promote economic and political reforms proved ineffectual. As a result on September 1, 1981, his regime was overthrown in a bloodless coup by General Andre Kolingba who led the country as head of the Military Committee for National Recovery (MCNR) for four years. In 1985, Kolingba dissolved the MCNR and named a new cabinet with increased civilian participation, signaling the beginning of a return to civilian rule. The process of democratization began with the creation of a new political party, the *Rassemblement Democratique Centrafricain* (RDC) and the drafting of a new constitution that was ratified through a national referendum. General Kolingba was sworn in as a constitutional president on November 29, 1986. The constitution established a National Assembly made up of fifty-two deputies, who were elected in July 1987.

Due to mounting political pressure, in 1991 President Kolingba announced the creation of a national commission to rewrite the constitution to promote a multiparty system. Multiparty presidential elections were conducted in 1992, but were later cancelled due to serious logistical and other irregularities. In the rescheduled election held in October 1993 Ange-Felix Patasse won a second-round victory. He was reelected for another six-year term in September 1999. Ange-Felix Patasse's civilian government was plagued by unrest, and in March 2003 his regime was deposed in a military coup led by General Francois Bozize, who established a transitional government. Though the government had the tacit support of civil society groups and the main parties, a wide field of candidates contested the municipal, legislative, and presidential elections held in March and May of 2005, in which General Bozize was affirmed as president. He was reelected in the 2011 elections that were widely viewed as having gross inaccuracies and discrepancies. The elected government did not fully control the countryside, where pockets of lawlessness persisted as a result of a militant group, Lord's Resistance Army (LRA).[25] By 2012, the Central African Republic entered into a year-long civil war which led to President Bozize fleeing the country.

In March 2013, under the leadership of Michel Djotodia, the Muslim rebel group, Sebeka, took over the government. Djotodia appointed himself as the president and suspended the constitution. However, by January 2014, against the background of international outcry over human rights violation, President Djotodia resigned from the presidency after establishing the National Transitional Council (NTC). On January 23, 2014, the NTC elected Catherine Samba-Panza as interim president; she defeated her political opponent Desire Colingba in a second round of voting with seventy-five votes to his fifty-three votes.[26] President Samba-Panza was supposed to serve until February 2015 when elections were scheduled. However, her term was extended until March 2016 owing to political instability.[27]

The Republic of Cameroon

French Cameroon became independent in 1960 as the Republic of Cameroon. The following year the southern portion of neighboring British Cameroon voted to merge with the new country to form the Federal Republic of Cameroon in 1972. However, the country has continued to face the challenges of democratic consolidation since 1982 when Paul Biya was elected.[28] After forty years as president, Biya retained a strong hold on Cameroon. His party, the Cameroon People's Democratic Movement (CPDM), controls the Senate, the National Assembly, and municipal councils by large majorities. As of the 2011 presidential elections, Biya defeated nearly two dozen opponents to claim 78 percent of the vote, which was widely viewed as tainted.[29]

Cameroon has a 180-seat National Assembly and established the 100-seat Senate in 2012; representatives serve five-year terms. In 2013, Cameroon held National Assembly elections, direct elections for municipal councilors, and long-delayed elections for its first Senate. The CPDM won fifty-six of the elected Senate seats, while the main opposition party, the Anglophone-led Social Democratic Front (SDF) won the remaining fourteen. Biya appointed an additional thirty senators of which three came from each of the country's ten regions. The CPDM took 148 assembly seats and won 305 of the country's 360 communes.[30]

In 2016, Cameroon faced several political, economic and security challenges such as youth unemployment, and aging political leadership as a result of the lack of an apparent successor to President Biya. In addition, the Northern Province which shares border with the North Eastern region of Nigeria, a major stronghold of terrorist group Boko Haram, has continued to contribute to security instability in Cameroon and neighboring Central African Republic

São Tomé and Príncipe

The Republic of São Tomé and Príncipe presents a different political challenge when compared to the democratic instability observed in the Central African Republic and Cameroon. São Tomé and Príncipe has been relatively free for approximately twenty years since 1995.[31] Portugal ruled the country beginning in the late 15th century. Though the country attained independence in 1975, democratic reforms were not instituted until the late 1980s. The country held its first free elections in 1991. However, as a result of frequent internal wrangling among the various political parties, the country experienced repeated change in leadership and four failed, non-violent coup attempts in 1995, 1998, 2003, and 2009. In 2012 the majority government of Prime Minister Patrice Trovoada was forced to leave office after a vote of no confidence by the three opposition parties. However, the 2014 legislative elections returned him to the prime ministership.[32] After the Independent Democratic Action party (ADI) defeated the governing Movement for the Liberation of São Tomé and Príncipe—Social Democratic Party in the 2014 parliamentary elections—the country remained stable in 2015.[33]

The challenge of democratic consolidation in the Central African subregion as in other SSA sub-regions has been almost elusive. For the most part the process of democratization has been shaped by a pendulum-like movement, whereby the region experienced moments of instability from 1973 until 2016.[34] For example, São Tomé and Príncipe was partly free (PF) from 1976 until 1978, not free (NF) from 1978 through 1989, and free (F) from 1991 through 2016.[35] Similarly, Cameroon was ranked partially free (PF) from 1973 through 1976; and ranked not free (NF) from 1977 through 2016.[36]

Along the foregoing lines, the IIAG scored the Central African region at an average of 41.2 points, making it a medium ranking. Though the governance level improved by + 11.2 score points,[37] overall, the IIAG time series data from 2005 through 2016 shows that all countries in the Central African Region achieved some improvement except for the Central African Republic, which is ranked among countries showing the most deteriorating trend in overall governance level in the past ten years.[38]

SUMMARY

The electoral trends in SSA provide an overview of democratic processes in African countries by sub-regions. The democratic gains of the late 1980s appear to have been threatened. The factors that led to the retreat in democratic gains are diverse, though there are some common threads. In several instances, the lack of government transparency, coups d'état, openness in government conduct, the personality cult of the presidency, increased pressure by the government to inhibit freedom of expression and the media, and weakness in the rule of law are profound factors that have stalled the progress for democracy. It is in this regard that Richard Joseph highlighted the challenges of the "frontier markets" which are countries that lack the reliable operating structures of emerging market countries, but which nonetheless yield high profits and show signs of sustained growth and improving economic governance. He identified countries such as Nigeria, Ghana, Mozambique, Tanzania, and Uganda[39] as frontier markets. This was the first time in decades that a positive flow of investment capital has occurred in these countries in sectors other than those devoted to the extraction of natural resources.

However, a retreat in democratic gains in countries such as Mauritania, São Tomé and Príncipe, and Guinea-Bissau, where coups were recently reported, and the institutionalization of political power in Kenya and Zimbabwe are common reminders of the cautious optimism that one must exercise in examining democratic trends in SSA.[40] In this regard, Larry Diamond evoked the argument that the counterbalance of the rule of law and the rule of person, in the presidency, has threatened democracy even in countries that appeared to have had long-standing political stability.[41] For example, countries such as Ghana, South Africa, Mali, and Senegal have shown an increased tendency toward autocratic rule.[42] Similarly, countries with less impressive democratic histories such as Chad, Ethiopia, and Eritrea have continued to confront challenges particularly in the areas of freedom of expression and protecting and maintaining the rule of law.[43]

An overview of recent electoral results in SSA provides a useful framework in which one can use to better understand democratic trends in SSA. Albeit at times these trends have become unpredictable and have resulted in changes that run counter to the democratic aspirations of the people.

NOTES

1. Constitutive Act of the African Union 2002. http://www.au2002.gov.za/docs/key_oau.

2. B. Guy Peters. *American Public Policy: Promise and Performance*, tenth edition (Los Angeles: CQ Press).
3. Freedom House Country Report on Ethiopia. http://www.freedomhouse.org/report/freedom-world/2012/ethiopia. Retrieved November 6, 2012.
4. Rene Lemarchand, "Foreign Policy Making in the Great Lakes," in Gilbert M. Khadiagala and Terrence Lyons (eds.), *African Foreign Policy: Power and Process* (Boulder: Lynne Rienner Publishers, 2001).
5. Freedomhouse.org: press release "Press Freedom Findings in Middle East and North Africa Disappointing after Earlier Hopeful Years," 1, Retrieved December 8, 2008.
6. Jreisat, *Globalism and Comparative Public Administration*, 5.
7. Ibid.
8. Ibid.
9. "CIA World Facts Book Background on Algeria." https://www.cia.gov/library/publications/the-world-factbook/geos/ag.html.
10. http://www.nytimes.com/interactive/2015/04/20/world/europe/surge-in-refugees-crossing-the-mediterranean-sea-maps.html?_r=0.
11. International Crisis Group. "Implementing Peace and Security Architecture: Architecture II Southern Africa Report," no. 191 (October 15, 2012). http://www.crisisgroup.org/en/regions/africa/southern-africa.aspx.
12. Mo Ibrahim Foundation, "2016 Ibrahim Index of African Governance: A Decade of African Governance 2006–2015," (2016): 20. High–71.0 and above, medium = high 54.0–70.9, medium 41.0–53.9, medium = low 23.0–40.9, low below 23.0.
13. Brian Raftopoulos and Ian Phimister, "Zimbabwe Now: The Political Economy of Crisis and Coercion," *Historical Materialism* 12, no. 4 (2004), 369
14. Lloyd M. Sachikonye, "Wither Zimbabwe? Crisis & Democratization," *Review of African Political* Economy 91 (2002), 18
15. "High Moon in Zimbabwe," *New African* (May 2008), 12–19.
16. Celia W. Dugger and Barry Bearak, "Mugabe Is Sworn In to Sixth Term After Victory in One-Candidate Runoff," *New York Times*, June 30, 2008.
17. "Freedom House Staus Change and Rating Change, Zimbabwe." https://freedomhouse.org/report/freedom-world/2016/zimbabwe. Retrieved September 9, 2016.
18. Mo Ibrahim Foundation, "A Decade of African Governance 2006–2015," 21
19. Ibid.
20. Ibid, 71.
21. Ibid.
22. "Central African Republic." http://www.britannica.com/EBchecked/topic/102127/Central-Africa. Retrieved November 3, 2012.
23. "Freedom House Sub-Saharan Africa." https://freedomhouse.org/regions/sub-saharan-africa. Retrieved September 11, 2016.
24. "Central Africa Region Political History." http://globaledge.msu.edu/Countries/Central-African-Republic/History. Retrieved from Global Edge.

25. "Central African Republic," *CIA Factbook*. https://www.CIAfactbook. Retrieved November 5, 2012.
26. "Freedom House Sub-Saharan Africa." https://freedomhouse.org/regions/su b-saharan-africa. Retrieved September 11, 2016.
27. "Central African Republic," *CIA Factbook*. https://www.cia.gov/librarypublic/ publications/the-worldfactbook/geos/ct.html. Retrieved September 11, 2016.
28. https://www.cia.gov/library/publications/the-world-factbook/geos/cm.html.
29. https:// freedom house.org/report/freedom-world/2016/Cameroon.
30. Ibid.
31. "Freedom House Sub-Saharan Africa." https://freedomhouse.org/regions/ sub-saharan-africa. Retrieved September 11, 2016.
32. https://www.cia.gov/library/publications/resources/the-world-factbook/geos/ tp.html.
33. Ibid.
34. "Freedom House Sub-Saharan Africa." https://freedomhouse.org/regions/su b-saharan-africa. Retrieved March 13, 2017.
35. Ibid.
36. Ibid.
37. "Ibrahim Index of African Governance," *A Decade of African Governance 2006–2015*, 71. The Ibrahim Index of Governance shows the following ranking for governance level in Central African Region: 71.0–above = high, 54.0–70.9 = medium = high, 41.0–53.9 = medium, 23.0–40.9 = medium = low, and below 23.0 = low.
38. Ibid., 18.
39. Richard Joseph, "Challenges of Frontier Region," *Journal of Democracy* 19, no. 2 (April 2008), 2–16.
40. Daniel N. Posner and Daniel Young, "Institutionalization of Political Power in Africa," *Journal of Democracy* 18, no. 3 (July 2007), 126–40.
41. Larry Diamond, "The Rule of Law versus the Big-man," *Journal of Democracy* 19, no. 2 (April 2008).
42. Joseph, "Challenges of Frontier Region," 2–16.
43. Freedom House, "Freedom in the World: Country Ratings 1972–2005." http:// www.FreedomHouse.Org; See also, Arch Puddington, "Freedom in the World 2007: Freedom Stagnation Amid Pushback Against Democracy," 5. http://www.freedom-house.org.

Chapter 4

Democracy and Economic Growth in Africa

Case Studies of South Africa and Ghana

Examining the relationship between democracy and economic growth is an important issue in most political economies including those of Africa. For this purpose, we examine the impact of democratic governance on economic growth using Ghana and South Africa as case studies in this chapter (to be followed by the case of Nigeria in the next chapter). South Africa and Ghana were selected because of their histories and their unique experiences in adopting political and economic reforms. Besides Liberia and Ethiopia, they are the two oldest independent states in Africa. Ghana was the second country to attain political independence in SSA from British colonial rule in 1957, following the independence of Sudan in 1956. Recently, Ghana has received notoriety from the international donor community for successful political and economic reforms. Since the 1980s, development agencies and scholars have perceived Ghana as being in the forefront of African socioeconomic development issues. Similarly, South Africa is one of the most recent countries to experience major political reforms toward democracy in Africa, especially after years of oppressive governance by the white apartheid regime. South Africa is also one of the BRICS countries (Brazil, Russia, India, China, and South Africa). These countries are members of an economic union that is considered emerging or third economic power.[1]

THE CASE OF SOUTH AFRICA

At the end of the nineteenth century most African states were under colonial rule. The European countries had self-appointed themselves through military aggression as rulers of the African continent whose natural and human resources they exploited to the fullest. However, the Europeans as far back as

1652 arrived in South Africa and eventually established various independent republics (the Cape of Good Hope, Natal, the Transvaal, and the Orange River Colony). The Transvaal and the Orange River Colony, dominated by the peoples of Dutch-German-French ancestry (or Boers), were called Boer Republics. The other colonies were dominated by English settlers. By the mid-1800s a struggle had ensued between the English and the Boers (who were later to be called Afrikaners) over control of the region's enormous resources. The struggle led to the Anglo-Boer war, which began around 1899 and lasted until 1902. It led to the loss of the independence of the Boer Republics, culminating with the integration of South Africa into the Commonwealth in 1910.

The British government eventually relieved itself from the daily responsibility of the colonial administration of South Africa, because South Africa's Commonwealth status offered Britain the same opportunities without the administrative responsibilities of colonial governance. This decision by the British had several social and political implications. It led to the manifestation of Afrikaner nationalism and placed the indigenous ethnic groups at the political mercy of Afrikaner groups.[2] Thus, by 1948 Afrikaner nationalism had formally been developed into what came to be known as apartheid or separate development. It expressed the determination of the Afrikaners to retain political, social, and economic control by employing the policy of apartheid. Apartheid was composed of four elements: (1) the forced separation of white and black South Africans; (2) the control of the movement and employment of black South Africans; (3) the establishment of reservations (or so-called homelands) for African ethnic groups; and (4) a white minority police state apparatus designed to control resistance from the black majority.[3]

However, after over 300 years of white domination of the country's majority black population, South Africa made a remarkable transition to democratic governance in 1994 as a result of global anti-apartheid political and economic sanctions by holding multi-ethnic elections that led to Nelson Mandela being elected the first indigenous president of the country.[4] Thus, South Africa, which emerged from the shadow of a liberation struggle and an oppressive and racist government, has negotiated two democratic constitutions and held five successful nationwide elections.[5]

Despite the democratic gains of the mid-1990s, national elections in South Africa have been hardly competitive because of the dominance of the African National Congress Party (ANC). The ANC's dominance in national elections is attributive to the support it receives from the national majorities. In this regard, the election of 1999 ushered in the Thabo Mbeki administration with 66 percent of the vote going to ANC. In 2004, Thabo Mbeki was reelected to a second term and ANC won 70 percent of the vote.

The democratic gains achieved after the historical election of 1994 were fully tested through a parliamentary vote of no confidence passed by the ANC party stalwarts on Mbeki's administration in October 2008. The vote of no confidence gave impetus for the rise of the ANC left wing alliance partners, the Congress of South African Trade Union (COSATU) and the Communist Party (SACP), which became frustrated by the poor social economic conditions of blacks in South Africa. Since the mid-1990s, the economy has shed over 500,000 jobs with economic growth at the rate of 3 percent and overall unemployment estimated at 23 percent.[6] The number of people receiving social welfare assistance has also increased from 2.5 million in 1995 to 12 million in 2007. As a result of the mounting social and economic crisis in South Africa, along with political pressure from opposition groups, such as COSTAU and SACP, Thabo Mbeki resigned from office in October 2008 and Koglema Motlanthe was chosen as the interim president by the South African General Assembly. Despite the political division in the ANC and the personal crisis of its leading candidate, Jacob Zuma, the ANC won the 2009 presidential election by 66.4 percent of the vote, down from 69.69 percent five years earlier.[7]

In light of the political dominance of the ANC, South Africa can be described as a one-party state. However, challenges from opposition groups and leadership crisis within the party are a threat to the ANC political dominance. Additionally, the Zuma administration has continued to experience similar social and economic challenges as the Mbeki administration. With rising unemployment, crime, political corruption, and xenophobia toward immigrants from other African states the democratic gains of the 1990s are steadily being threatened.

THE CASE OF GHANA

Since independence in 1957, Ghana has experienced nine changes in government, which include four military coups. Economic mismanagement has been the major source of the political conflict in Ghana. This mismanagement has resulted in economic stagnation and wide disparities in resource distribution among interest groups, which often leads to political unrests.[8]

Thus, an overview of regime changes in postcolonial Ghana provides a broader context in which one can better understand the types of economic policies that have emerged from one period to another. For example, during the early period of independence, Ghana's first president, Kwame Nkrumah (who ruled from 1957 to 1966) pursued a socialist economic agenda. The country at that time relied on revenues from cocoa exports to pursue industrial development. However, the decline in the price of this primary commodity and rapid urban industrial development, which depended on imported capital-intensive inputs, created an economic imbalance. This further drove the administration into acute dependency on imported capital-intensive products. The ensuing economic crises led to the demise of the Nkrumah regime through the 1966 military coup led by Colonel Emmanuel Kwasi Kotoka and Major Akwasi Amankwa Afrifa. This coup brought into power Lieutenant-General Ankrah under the guidance of the National Liberation Council (NLC).[9] However, on April 2, 1969, General Ankrah was forced out of office in an internal power struggle in the armed forces and was succeeded by General Afrifa as Chairman of the NLC.[10]

The NLC with the support of the military had three main policy objectives: (1) restoring budget stability, (2) addressing the imbalance in foreign trade, and (3) consolidating foreign debts in an attempt to better manage rising debts. The government curtailed public spending and enacted severe restrictions on imports and external borrowing. Though these measures were effective in reducing inflation by 50 percent between 1966 and 1967, they had no impact on the existing macroeconomic problems of high unemployment and slow economic growth.[11]

Ghana also encountered economic problems between 1971 and 1972, which led to increased public dissent and ushered in the National Redemption Council and the Supreme Military Council of General Ignatius Kutu Acheampong in 1972.[12] General Acheampong's regime, backed by trade unionists, reverted to the socialist economic policy introduced by Nkrumah at the time of independence. The regime initiated self-reliant development programs, which, on one hand, encouraged strict regulation of imports and, on the other hand, hardly provided any incentives for exports. These programs also emphasized reliance on the use of domestic resources. One such program was called "Operation Feed Yourself," designed to make the country self-sufficient in food production. These programs, which were afflicted by gross public corruption and economic hardships, provided the impetus for another military coup.[13]

The coup brought into power General Frederick Akuffo as Chairman of the Supreme Military Council (SMC). Although he began the process of Ghana's transition to civilian rule,[14] his regime was short lived when it was overthrown in another military coup led by Flight Lieutenant Jerry Rawlings on June 4, 1979. Shortly thereafter, an election was held on September 24, 1979, bringing into power President Hilla Limann of The People's National Party (PNP). The Limann administration pursued monetary policies prescribed by the International Monetary Fund (IMF), which encouraged: (1) agricultural production to increase export earnings; (2) reduction of budget deficits; (3) economic stabilization measures that increased cocoa producer prices; and (4) currency devaluation.[15]

Nevertheless, these economic measures, which received little support from the middle class, led to the second coup of the Armed Forces Revolutionary Council (AFRC) in 1981 by Flight Lieutenant Jerry Rawlings. Rawlings initially pursued a socialist economic development policy, but later abandoned it for the liberal economic recovery policy that consisted of the structural adjustment program (SAP) under the auspices of the World Bank and the IMF.[16] Although Ghana gained notoriety from the international donor community for successful political and economic reforms, the overall performance of the Ghanaian economy under the SAP was to the contrary. Despite projected annual growth of 8 percent in export volume between 1987 and 1990, macroeconomic performance reflected unfavorable external terms of trade, relative lack of export diversity, and limited scope for further import compression, leading to a dependence on concessional aid flows. Economic growth was negative during the early phase of the 1980s and averaged less than 2 percent during the rest of that period. The consequences of these economic conditions were a decline in wages and further deterioration in basic social infrastructures, such as health and educational services.[17]

Following the 1981 coup, Rawlings remained a dominant personality in Ghanaian politics for another twenty years. During this period, the constitutional amendment of 1992 limited the presidential term of office to two four-year terms. Rawlings who ran on the platform of the National Democratic Congress (NDC) and won the 1992 elections by 53 percent of the electoral votes compared to his closest rival Adu-Bohaen of the New Patriotic Party (NPP) who had won 30 percent of the electoral votes. In the 1996 elections, the NPP and the Peoples Convention Party (PCP) developed a coalition with the hope of unseating Rawlings from the presidency but their effort did not bring about the needed political victory. Rawlings won the elections with 56 percent of the electoral votes while the opposition candidate John Kuffor had only 41 percent.[18] Thereafter, in a remarkable peaceful political transition process, John Kuffor of the NPP won a highly contested presidential election in 2000, after a runoff with the NDC party candidate John Evans Atta-Mills.[19]

The 2000 election began a new era in Ghana's efforts toward democratic consolidation. Thus, after eight years of President Kuffor's administration, some of the ethos of democracy, free and competitive elections, were tested in the 2008 national election. The first round of voting which began in December 7, 2008, was inconclusive because the candidate from the ruling party, New Patriotic Party (NPP), Nana Akufo-Addo, and the candidate for the opposition party, NDC, John Atta-Mills, had less than the constitutionally required minimum of 51 percent of the vote. The outcome of the highly competitive first round of election led to a runoff election on December 28, 2008. On January 2, 2009, John Atta-Mills, the NDC presidential candidate, was declared the winner after garnering 50.2 percent of the vote compared to

49.8 percent for Nana Akufo-Addo. The electoral process and the successful political transition after the 2008 election received wide support from the international community and are seen as an example for the rest of Africa. US president, Barrack Obama, paid an official visit to the country in 2009, a further attestation of the country's successful democratic governance.

The democratic gains associated with Ghana were again tested when Ghana's President John Atta-Mills died on July 24, 2012, after a prolonged illness. His Vice President, John Dramani Mahama, constitutionally replaced him as un-elected president for six months. Thereafter, on December 7, 2012, John Draman Mahama, the incumbent representing NDC, won a contested election on his own merits against the opposition candidate Nana Akufo-Addo, representing the NPP. John Dramani Mahama of the NDC received 50.70 percent of the electoral vote, and the opposition Nana Akufo-Addo had 47.74 percent of the vote.

The 2012 election was highly contested and was reported free and fair by international election observers such as the AU and the UN. Contrarily, opposition forces led by Nana Akufo-Addo of the NPP felt that the elections were mired by irregularities. The primary contention of NPP was that election workers had improperly signed off on ballot forms which placed the incumbent John Draman Mahama at an advantage. Consequently, NPP filed a petition to the Supreme Court challenging the results of the elections after President John Draman Mahama was inaugurated on January 7, 2013. After a six-month hearing, the Supreme Court did not find a sufficient cause to order a new election. To this end, the political anxiety created by the NPP's challenge of the 2012 election and the civil outcome of the court case shows that democracy is progressing more in Ghana than in many other African countries.

This is evident by the fact that constitutional democracy was consolidated when all actors after the 2012 presidential elections in Ghana subjected themselves to the resolution of election conflict by following specific laws, procedures and institutions sanctioned by the new democratic process instead of resorting to political conflict as was the case in countries such as Kenya.[20] The peaceful political transition after the presidential elections of 2016 was a testimony of the extent of democratic consolidation in Ghana. President Nana Akuffor-Addo, representing the opposition party, won the election by 53 percent of the vote and the incumbent, former President Mahama garnered only 44 percent of the electoral votes.[21]

THE EMPIRICAL EVIDENCE

Given the international notoriety that South Africa and Ghana received with respect to their political reforms, we tested the impact of these reforms on the economic performance in these countries. We also tested and compared the impact of government size, democracy, and openness of the economy on economic growth in the two countries. The estimated results of the impact of various political economy variables on economic growth are presented in appendix A.

The estimated effects of the government size are negative in nearly all models except one in the case of Ghana, where it is positive (see appendix A). However, only one of these estimates is significant. This is in the case of South Africa where, on the average, a percent increase in government size reduced economic growth by about 0.5 percent. In the case of Ghana, the results suggest that growth in the size of government had no impact on economic growth over the period under review.

Estimates of the impact of the political freedom are significantly negative in the case of Ghana, but had not effects in the case of South Africa. However, in the case of South Africa, the estimated effects of the not-free status were significantly negative and lower than the partly free status. In the case of Ghana, there was no difference in economic growth during period when the country was ranked partly free and not free. Thus, unlike the Ghanaian economy, the South African economy appears to have benefited moderately from political liberalization. This difference in the impact of political liberation in the two countries will be discussed later.

Growth in the size of government and political freedom appear to affect economic growth. Growth in government size slows down economic growth, while political freedom promotes economic growth. According to economic theory, government is inefficient in the provision of Pigovian goods and services and tends to create distortions in the economy through its taxing, spending, and rent-seeking policies. Growth in government also tends to crowd out investment, which is necessary for economic growth. These inefficiencies and distortions retard economic growth as indicated by the negative estimated impact of the government size variable in this study. The degree of political freedom also has a positive impact on economic growth. Economic growth requires, among other factors, a condition of political freedom in which there is mass participation in the decision making process, which can promote efficiency in the use of capital.

So, why did the South African economy benefit from political liberalization while the Ghanaian economy did not during the early years of such reform? With Ghana being classified as politically free for only a few years—1980 to 1982—the country did not have much experience with political liberalization. On the other hand, while the apartheid policy in South Africa prevented blacks from participating in the democratic process, South Africa had much experience with democratic governance among its ruling whites, and the country as a whole had also been experiencing political freedom since the multi-ethnic election of 1994 which led to the election of its first indigenous president, Nelson Mandela. Moreover, despite fifteen years of the SAP in Ghana (1983–1998), domestic private entrepreneurs in the country did not respond with increased investment. According to a recent study by Nicholas Amponsah, an important reason for the lukewarm private sector response to the SAP is the poor institutional environment, and the fundamental problem of institutional decay. As the World Bank's country study concluded, "today, Ghanaians still believe that doing business entails major political risk." In 1997/1998 survey of 433 private entrepreneurs, 60 percent said that they have no confidence that the state will enforce the rule of law. The institutional environment of the country may be seen as insecure by most critical actors, such as domestic private entrepreneurs, whose cooperation is crucial in the effectiveness of the reform program. Attempts at political reforms have not improved entrepreneurial confidence to increase investment for economic growth and development. Thus, as this study has found, political reforms have not had a significantly positive impact on the economy of Ghana.

SUMMARY

Since the breakup of the Soviet Union, democratic institutions have been flourishing across the globe. The chapter assessed the impact of such political reforms in Africa, focusing on Ghana and South Africa. These two countries are the focus of this study because of the international notoriety they received for their progress in promoting democratic governance.

The results show that the promotion of democratic institutions seems to have had significant positive impact on economic growth in South Africa. Periods of political freedom were positively associated with economic growth, while periods when such freedom was circumscribed or proscribed were negatively associated with economic growth. On the other hand, growth in government size had a negative impact. Economic growth declined at 50 percent of the rate of increase in the size of government. Thus, a politically free environment with a limited role of government in economic life contributed to economic growth in South Africa.

In the case of Ghana, promoting political freedom had no positive impact on economic growth. The rate of economic growth declined during periods of political freedom compared to periods when such freedom was abridged. Growth in the size of government, labor, and investment also did not have a positive impact on economic growth. The results are therefore contrary to the view of the international donor community that political and economic reforms contributed to economic performance in Ghana.

Over the sample period, from 1960 to 1998, Freedom House classified Ghana as politically free in only 1980/1982. During the rest of the period the country was classified as either partly free or not free. Since independence in 1957, Ghana has had four military coups, which suggest that most of Ghana's political life has been dominated by authoritarian regimes. Thus, the country had not had much experience with political liberalization to realize its benefits on economic growth.

NOTES

1. World Economic Forum, "Five Factors Limiting the Impact of BRICS Nations." https://www.weforum.org/agenda/2015/07/5-factors-limiting-the-impact-of-the-brics-nations/.
2. Edmond J. Keller and Donald Rothschild, *Africa in the New International Order* (Boulder, CO: Lynne Reiner Publishers, 1996).
3. Leslie Rubin and Brian Weinstein, *Introduction to African Politics* (New York: Holt Publishing Company, 1977).
4. The election of 1994 brought an end to the domination of the white National Party and the policy of apartheid, which was instituted in 1948.
5. Robert Mates, "South Africa: Democracy Without the People," *Journal of Democracy* 13, no. 1 (January 2002), 23–26.
6. Mark Reviser, "Time of Reckoning," *BBC Focus* (2009), 16.
7. Reviser, "Time of Reckoning," 18.
8. Ho-Wong Jeong, "Economic Reform and Democratic Transition in Ghana," *World Affairs* 160, no. 4 (1998), 218–31.
9. Ho-Wong Jeong, "Economic Reform and Democratic Transition in Ghana."; M. S. Prabhakara, "A History of Coups," *Frontline* 18, no. 2 (2001), 1–5.
10. Prabhakara, "A History of Coups."
11. Jeong, "Economic Reform and Democratic Transition in Ghana."
12. Ibid.
13. Ibid.
14. Prabhakara, "A History of Coups," 1–5.
15. Jeong, "Economic Reform and Democratic Transition in Ghana."; Eboe Hutchful, "Reconstructing Civil Military Relations and the Collapse of Democracy in Ghana, 1979–81," *African Affairs* 96, no. 385 (1997), 535–60.
16. Jeong, "Economic Reform and Democratic Transition in Ghana."; Kwame Arthur-Boafo, "Ghana: Structural Adjustment, Democratization, and the Politics of Continuity," *African Studies Review* 42, no. 2 (September 1999), 45.
17. Simon Commander, John Howell, and Wayo Siena, "Ghana: 1983–87," in Simon Commander (ed.), *Structural Adjustment & Agriculture: Theory and Practice in Africa and Latin America* (London: Overseas Development Institute, 1989).
18. Jeong, "Economic Reform and Democratic Transition in Ghana," 218–31.
19. Daniel Smith, "Ghana's 2000 Elections: Consolidating Multiparty Democracy," *Electoral Studies* 21 (2002), 473–533; Boadi E. Gyimah, "A Peaceful Turnover in Ghana," *Journal of Democracy* 12, no. 2 (April 2001), 103–17.

20. A. Asante and E. B. Asare, "Ghana 2012 Election Petition and Its Outcome: A Giant Leap Towards Democratic Consolidation," *Journal of Political Science and Public Affairs* 4, no. 196 (2016), 2–6. doi:10.4172/2332-0761.1000196.

21. BBC Africa, "Ghana Election: Opposition Leader Akufor-Addo Declared Winner," December 9, 2016. https//:bbc.com. Retrieved February 17, 2017.

Chapter 5

Government Size, Political Freedom, and Economic Growth

The Case Study of Nigeria

Although Nigeria is not among the countries that have been ranked free in Africa for decades, it is, however, one of the countries that have embarked on the pursuit of democratic market institutions. However, the political process in pursuing such institutions has been turbulent. During most of the years after independence, Nigeria has been under military rule. During its fifty-seven years of independence (1960–2017), the country has experienced twenty-nine years of military rule and sixteen years of civilian rule.

After nearly six decades of independence, determining the impact of Nigeria's democratic engagement as well as its governance structure on economic growth is important. More specifically, this chapter analyzes the Nigerian political economy by assessing the impacts of government size, political freedom, and openness of the economy on economic growth, as done in the cases of Ghana ad South Africa in the previous chapter.

POLITICAL BACKGROUND

On October 1, 1960, Nigeria became an independent state under a parliamentary system of government. Like most African countries, Nigeria has continued to struggle with what appears to be an elusive goal for political and economic freedoms even after more than forty-five years of independence. The country has experienced numerous military coups and counter coups and has survived a secessionist civil war. The attainment of political independence does not seem to have transformed the state because the indigenous elites that replaced the colonial administrators have failed to implement policies to move the country forward politically and economically. The indigenous elites inherited a state that was not designed to cater to the needs of the

Nigerian people; yet, these elites were content with the political structures designed by the colonialists.[1] According to Wale Olaitan,

> The fact that the state, given its enormous resources, was the most secured and quickest source of accumulation after independence meant that politics as a struggle for the control of the instruments of the state became a fierce battle. Many people became interested in the state, not because it was useful for the generality of the society but because it could be exploited for personal and material gains.[2]

It is against this background that we examine the pendulum of political transition in Nigeria—civilian to military to civilian to military . . .

POLITICAL TRANSITIONS

Military rule in Nigeria began with a coup d'état led by Major Chukkwuma Nzeogwu in January 1966, six years after independence. This coup led to the demise of the first parliamentary government in the country. A couple of perspectives have been advanced as the raison d'etre for the coup. First is the position that the coup plotters were disillusioned with the level of corruption and inefficiency of the political elites.[3] Second, it was alleged that the coup was designed to overthrow the dominant northern political elites.[4] Despite these reasons, the coup was not successful, because a few military officers of eastern descent, along with a highly respected major general, Aguiyi Ironsi, thwarted the coup attempt. However, the civilian political elites yielded power to the military because it appeared that a civil war was eminent if political power remained with a civilian government.[5]

The political elites from the north appeared to have been the primary target of the coup, even though senior members of parliament from the Western and mid-west regions, such as Chief Samuel L. Akintola and Finance Minister Festus Okotieboh, respectively, were also assassinated. The federal prime minister, Sir Abubakar Tafawa Balewa, and a senior member of parliament from the north, Sir Ahmadu Bello, were both assassinated, while senior members of parliament from the east and mid-west escaped assassination attempts.

In July 1966, a second coup ensued. This coup was organized by northern military officers who had become angered by the death of several members of the political elites from their region during the January 1966 coup. The northern coup plotters targeted mostly Igbo military officers assigned to the north, claiming that these officers had benefited from the first coup. This conflict would later have significant impact on the political future of Nigeria—the attempt by the military governor of the east, Lieutenant Colonel Chukwu

Emeka Ojukwu, to lead a secessionist effort of the Biafran state from the Federal Republic of Nigeria.[6]

Following the July 1966 coup and the assassination of Major General Ironsi, northern military leaders began to call for the secession of the north from Nigeria. However, after receiving several appeals from the political elites, the military leaders withheld their plan to secede. Nevertheless, they agreed to keep their military units in Lagos, the federal capital, with the understanding that Lieutenant Colonel Yakubu Gowon, the army chief of staff and the most senior officer of Middle Belt origin, would assume office as the head of state. Rioting later broke out in Northern Nigeria, leading to ethnic violence against Igbos and consequently their mass exodus back to the east.

The SMC's decision to appoint Gowon as head of state and the continuous killing of Igbos were factors that ignited the Nigerian Civil War in 1967. The east, under the leadership of Major General Ojukwu, established the Biafran Republic in direct opposition to the federal structure that was dominated by northern military officers with support from military officers from the west and mid-west. After three years of intense fighting, the civil war came to an end in January 1970, when General Ojukwu fled the country for asylum in Cote d'Ivoire, and Lieutenant Colonel Effiong, the Biafran field commander, surrendered to the federal government.[7] The head of state after the war, General Yakubu Gowon, promised on October 1, 1970, to return the country to civilian rule by 1976. Four years later, he reneged on his promise by promulgating a military decree to extend his military rule indefinitely.[8]

In 1975, Murtala Mohammed assumed power as head of state through a military coup that ousted General Yakubu Gowon. Mohammed promised to return Nigeria to a democratically elected government by October 1, 1979. To this end, the administration embarked upon several programs to facilitate the political transition toward a civilian government. For example, new states and local governments were created, and a new constitution was drafted. However, the process of political transition faced a setback when Murtala Mohammed was assassinated in a coup by a group of army officials on February 13, 1976.

General Olusegun Obasanjo became the next head of state and continued with most of Murtala Mohammed's policies, especially the promise to return the country to a civilian government by 1979. The Obasanjo administration embarked upon the drafting of a new constitution that changed the parliamentary system of government to an American-style democratic republic. A Federal Election Commission was also established to provide the framework for political participation in the 1979 general elections.

After a closely contested election in 1979, Alhaji Shehu Shagari, a northerner, was elected president. The Shagari administration faced major economic challenges. In the 1980s, Nigeria's oil revenue plummeted by 73 percent from US$28.1 billion in 1980 to US$7.6 billion in 1982. At the same time, Nigeria's imports amounted to a billion dollars a month[9] and its external and internal debt rose astronomically. Internal public debt increased by 72 percent from $8.5 billion in 1979 to $29.6 billion in 1983, while the external debt was estimated at $14.13 billion during this period.[10] President Shagari's failure to address the pending economic crisis would later lead to the demise of his administration through a military coup in the early part of December 1983.

In the presidential election held in 1983, President Shagari was reelected for a second term of office. However, shortly after the election, Shagari was overthrown in a military coup on December 31, 1983, and Muhammadu Buhari became the next head of state. The Buhari administration promised to address the economic crisis plaguing the country. With this in mind, the administration forged ahead with the adoption of the 1982 Stabilization Act of the previous administration, a policy that was consistent with the IMF's recommendations to the Shagari administration. The policy recommendations of the fund laid strong emphasis on reducing public expenditures, monetary controls, and import restrictions. The Buhari administration attempted to implement some of these recommendations by reducing the budget deficit from $8.2 billion in 1983 to $3.8 billion in 1984, and by reducing government services by 40 percent during the same period. The administration, like its predecessors, did not fully implement the IMF's so-called SAP. Instead, most of its efforts focused on the passage of draconian military decrees to address corruption and, in some cases, to humiliate political opposition groups. For example, Decree No. 4 was passed for the preventive detention of opposition groups on security grounds, while Decree No. 2 proscribed all demonstrations, processions, and unauthorized meetings.[11]

On August 27, 1985, Ibrahim Babangida assumed the office of president through a military coup against a background of a deadlock between the IMF and the Buhari regime on the Fund's conditionality over a $2.5 billion Extended Fund Facility (EFF) loan. The Babangida administration promised to address the country's economic crisis and to break the deadlock between the IMF and the Buhari administration. While the administration began the process by encouraging a national debate on whether or not to accept IMF loans, it simultaneously engaged in secret discussions with the IMF on securing an adjustment package. A National Economic Emergency Program was also promulgated to, *inter alia*, introduce a general reduction in salaries, ranging from 2 percent to 20 percent, for both civilian and military employees. Labor unions bitterly criticized this policy because the administration failed to seek their opinion before its implementation.[12] The administration's actions were further denounced by professional groups such as the Manufacturer's

Association of Nigeria (MAN), academics, and some military personnel, especially for its secret discussions with the IMF and its willingness to accept the fund's conditions.

In response, the government announced that Nigeria would reject the IMF loan and instead would develop a homegrown adjustment program.[13] However, the policy that emerged conformed very closely with the IMF's conditions. Thus, on June 27, 1986, the Babangida administration announced the commencement of a structural adjustment program, with the major objective being the removal of the perceived over-valuation of the Nigerian currency, the naira, through the establishment of a foreign exchange bidding scheme under a second-tier foreign exchange market.[14]

The adoption of the SAP was unpopular. In an attempt to manage increasing dissentions, the Babangida administration promised to return power to a civilian government. The administration introduced a political transition program in 1988 with the intention of returning political power to a civilian government by 1993. The government carefully orchestrated the transition program by forming two political parties, the National Republican Convention (NRC) and the Social Democratic Party (SDP), and imposing them on the Nigerian people. However, after five years of planning and spending an estimated US$97.3 million,[15] President Babangida nullified the results of the 1993 presidential election, declaring that the election results were flawed and that new elections would be held later to return the country to civilian rule. According to the 1993 election results, Alhaji Moshood Abiola, the SDP presidential aspirant from the Southwestern region, won the presidency, winning nineteen of the thirty states.[16]

The annulled election drew strong opposition from the general public, human rights groups, and even some members of the military. As political opposition intensified, the government, in January 1993, established a political transition committee and appointed a Yoruba industrialist, Ernest Shonekan, to chair the committee. He was assigned the task of supervising what was coined as the military "Disengagement Program." On August 26, 1993, Shonekan was named interim head of state after General Babangida resigned in response to intense political opposition. The Shonekan transition government, however, came to an abrupt end in November 1993 when General Sani Abacha seized power through a military coup.[17] The Abacha military regime, like its predecessors, offered a similar pitch of completing a political transition program that would usher in a civilian government by 1995. However, the new government focused its efforts on persecuting political opposition groups and perceived opponents, some of whom were imprisoned or killed. For example, Chief Moshood Abiola, the winner of the June 12, 1993, election, and General Yar' Adua, a presidential aspirant, were both imprisoned for criticizing and defying the Abacha administration. Both later died in prison. The administration also targeted human rights activists, such as Saro Wiwa, the leader of the Ogonni group and a renowned writer, who was imprisoned and killed for opposing the administration's policies in the oil-producing delta states.

In the economic area, the Abacha administration made no radical departure from the broad economic principles under the SAP program. The administration's 1994 budget highlighted the following economic objectives: (1) a balanced budget firmly anchored in fiscal discipline and the abolition of deficit financing; (2) exchange rate stabilization and the reduction of the high incidence of capital flight; (3) the rationalization of interest rates to stem the decline of the real sector; and (4) the implementation of effective strategies to reduce debt service on domestic commitments, with the hope of obtaining debt relief from external creditors.[18]

Despite indications by the Abacha administration that the 1994 budget would address the economic hardship under SAP, economic indicators suggested otherwise. For example, nominal interest rates remained at the 1990 rate of 21 percent. The fixing of interest rates had served no purpose other than to provide cheap naira to buy foreign exchange, which further led to the decline in the value of the naira. The Abacha administration maintained its predecessor's commitment to the SAP policy of deregulation and safeguarding the integrity of market forces.[19]

However, the Abacha regime came to an unexpectedly abrupt end as a result of his mysterious death in May 1998. With his death, the military rallied around General Abdulsalam Abubakar who assumed power as head of the Provincial Ruling Council. After the completion of a year-long political transition program, General Abubakar handed political power over to the civilian government of President Olusegun Obasanjo on February 27, 1999. With the completion of his first term in office, President Olusegun Obasanjo was reelected in 2003 for a final term of office that ended in 2007.

During his two terms in office, and what appeared as the commitment of the Nigerian presidency to democracy and transparency, President Obasanjo and some of his political supporters at the national and state levels reverted to autocratic tendencies that were common practices under past military administrations. For instance, the president had planned to extend his term in office through a constitutional amendment that would have led to a third term. However, the Nigerian public, approximately 84 percent, and Western interests, especially the European Union (EU), and the United States, found the plan to extend the term of the presidency as anti-democratic.[20] The plan also received staunch opposition from the Nigerian General Assembly, especially the Senate.[21] The plan to elongate the presidency by the Obasanjo administration failed in the Nigerian Senate because the proponents of the plan could not acquire the two-third votes needed for such constitutional amendment.[22]

Subsequently, the 2006 Presidential elections, in light of alleged electoral malpractices, ushered in the administration of Umar Yaradua in 2007. The 2006 election would become a watershed in the political history of Nigeria because it was the first time that a democratic elected civilian government would hand over power to another civilian government.[23]

The Yaradua administration was short lived because of his fragile health. His prolong illness prompted the national assembly to declare Vice President Goodluck Jonathan as the acting president. Vice President Goodluck Jonathan was later confirmed constitutionally as the president, after of the death of President Yaradua on May 5, 2010. On April 9, 2011, President Goodluck Jonathan was elected the president of Nigeria for a four-year term after garnering close to 59 percent of the electoral votes of the 2011 national elections.[24]

Given the pendulum of political change in Nigeria, the country has been faced with several challenges, such as human trafficking, arms proliferation, ethno-religious conflict, and corruption.[25] But the greatest of these challenges is the threat by the Boko Haram Islamic militant group, which is literarily translated from the Hausa language as "Western Education is bad."[26] The group is held together by its support for the Sharia and its desire to see the implementation for full Sharia in Nigeria. Thus, the emergence of Boko Haram has led to a series of bomb attacks on Christians, Muslim clerics, politicians, and traditional leaders[27] However, it was the suicide bombing of the United Nation headquarters in Abuja that drew international attention to the activities of the group in Nigeria, and the concern by international observers that it may be receiving support from Al-Qaeda.[28] Additionally, Boko Haram has been kidnapping citizens, especially the one involving about 300 school girls. The threat posed by Boko Haram terrorist activities and the endemic political corruption in Nigeria is a major challenge to the stability of Nigeria. It is in this context, that the Nigerian Nobel Laureate, Wole Yinka, asserts, "When you get a situation where a bunch of people can go into a place of worship and open fire through the windows you have reached a certain dismal watershed in the life of the nation."[29]

After a protracted eight years of social, political, and economic upheaval under the People Democratic Party (PDP) Goodluck Jonathan administration, Nigeria appeared to be ready for a major political change that could very well consume the country from the crisis that had mired the Jonathan administration. The 2015 presidential election in Nigeria pitted the candidate of the major opposition party, the All Progressive Congress (APC), Muhammadu Buhari, a former military dictator in the 1980s, against the incumbent Goodluck Jonathan. On April 1, 2015, Muhammadu Buhari was ushered in as a president after a landmark election. First, this was the first time in Nigeria's fifty-five years of independence that an opposition presidential candidate would defeat an incumbent. Second, the incumbent president, Goodluck Jonathan, was defeated by a landslide of 2.5 million votes. Lastly, President Goodluck Jonathan conceded peacefully to Mohammed Buhari, a fete that is atypical in Nigerian political history. Thus, despite the ills of his administration, Goodluck Jonathan emerged as a political hero.[30]

At his inauguration on May 29, 2015, President Buhari reiterated his multiple campaign promises to fight corruption and the threat of Boko Haram terrorism. As a result, in his first hundred days in office he established a presidential inquiry to address political corruption and other forms of public graft. He also began the restructuring of the Nigerian military with the dismissal of some senior members of the armed forces and the appointment of new officers to move the military in a strategic direction. Along these lines, he entered into partnership with major powers such as the United States and Germany to combat terrorism. The Buhari administration has also engaged in regional security alliances with countries such as Cameroon, Chad, and Niger in the fight against Boko Haram. These alliances and the military makeover have the potential of repositioning the Nigerian military as a regional leader in the fight against terrorism.[31]

The challenge for the consolidation of democracy in Nigeria under the current political dispensation would be further tested by the ability of the Buhari administration to control a declining economy that was sparked by the declining global price of Nigeria's major export, crude oil. Albeit, the Buhari administration canvassed for the 2014 presidential election with the promise to end corruption and address security problems, as recent development in Nigeria indicated that the fight against public corruption was been fought selectively. Members of the president's APC party were hardly investigated or prosecuted for their present and past corrupt practices. At the same time, security issues continued to loom large because of the re-emergence of the delta region militants to target Nigeria's oil pipelines with explosives.[32] Invariably, the security issues adversely affected the economy, because the targeted oil pipelines led to the reduction in Nigeria's oil production capacity by half.[33]

THE ECONOMIC BACKGROUND

Since its independence in 1960, Nigeria has experienced mixed economic performance. The economy experienced an unprecedented boom in the early 1960s and the early 1970s. During these periods, the growth rate of GDP per capita ranged from 2 percent to 14 percent. However, by the 1980s, the country was plunged into economic crisis, stemming largely from two main factors—economic mismanagement and emphasis on revenues from the oil boom at the expense of the agricultural production. The oil boom of the 1970s and the early 1980s brought about a major windfall that consequently led to less priority being accorded to the agricultural sector, which was once a vital part of the Nigerian economy. In the early 1970s, the non-oil sector, which generated about 75 percent of Nigeria's total revenue, appeared to have been neglected since the oil boom period of the middle 1970s, such that it only contributed 22.5 percent of the total revenue in 1975. Its contributions to total revenue dropped further to 18.9 percent in 1980, increased again to 25.3 percent in 1985, and fell to16.1 percent in 1992. On the other hand, the oil sector presently contributes close to 95 percent of export revenues.[34]

The global and domestic dimensions of Nigeria's reliance on oil are manifested in its external debt crisis, which began during the oil boom of the 1970s. Nigeria's external debt, which is estimated at over $30 billion, has continued to rise because windfalls from oil exports during the 1970s and 1980s were squandered on politically motivated projects, such as the Ajaokuta Steel Plant. The plant cost over US$6 billion but is yet to produce any steel.[35] At the same time, the country continued to borrow money from international lending institutions, such as the IMF and World Bank, under stringent conditions, with the servicing costs of the foreign debt exceeding 70 percent of Nigeria's annual export earnings. Nigeria has continued to spend most of its scarce foreign reserves to service external debt. The country spent $1.9 billion in 2000, $2.13 billion in 2001, and $1.5 billion in 2002 to service its external debts.[36] Consequently, Nigeria, as a borrower, does not possess the economic leverage for favorable balance-of-payments since most of its export earnings are used to service debts.[37]

Despite Nigeria's increasing oil revenue and debt burden, the size of the government has remained relatively small. When measured as the share of government spending in GDP, the size of government ranged from a minimum of 3 percent in the early 1960s to a maximum of 35 percent in 2000. Besides the year 2000, government size did not exceed 16 percent in any other years. The mean size of the government was 10 percent over the sample period, 1960 to 2000. (See summary statistics in appendix A.) Thus, over the years, the size of government in Nigeria ranged from small to moderate when compared to those of other countries. Using comparable international macroeconomic data, published by Robert Summer and Alan Heston,[38] we provided examples of countries with small and large government sizes. The smallest government size (i.e., share of government expenditure in GDP of 10 percent or less) was found in countries such as Hong Kong, Japan, Korea, Luxembourg, Mauritius, Nigeria, Singapore, and Switzerland. The largest government size (i.e., share of government expenditure in GDP over 25 percent) was found in countries such as Algeria, Bulgaria, China, Cuba, Hungary, India, Israel, Jordan, Syria, and Ukraine.

The small-to-moderate size of government in Nigeria raises concerns about the country's public spending. With increasing oil revenues and external debts as sources of government spending on one hand, and declining economic growth on the other, the share of government spending in GDP should have been high enough to put Nigeria in the highest government size category. Thus, the small government size is not consistent with increasing government revenue and declining rate of economic growth in Nigeria. The small size of government suggests that government spending in Nigeria has not been fully accounted for, and/or government revenue from oil and debt may not have been spent on public projects. The small size of government may also indicate corruption in the Nigerian government.

The Nigerian economy is also beset by the twin problems of mismanagement and corruption by public officials under both military and civilian regimes. Since 1996, Transparency International, an international nongovernmental organization devoted to combating corruption, has annually ranked countries in terms of the degree to which corruption is perceived to exist among public officials and politicians in countries around the world.[39] Using surveys that ask questions in line with the misuse of public power for private benefit with a focus, for example, on bribe-taking by public officials in public procurement, Transparency International constructs a corruption indicator called the Corruption Perception Index (CPI). Over the period 1999 to 2003, Nigeria was ranked as the most corrupt country in the world in 2000, and the second most corrupt country in 1999, as well as in 2001, 2002, and 2003.[40] In 2014 the CPI for Nigeria shows that the country is ranked 136 out of 175 countries in regard to public sector corruption.[41]

The level of corruption in Nigeria seems not to have declined. Instead it has grown to an unprecedented level. For instance, under Presidential Goodluck Jonathan administration, the former governor of the Nigerian Central Bank, now the traditional Emir of Kano, Mr. Lamido Sanusi alleged that well over $49 billion of oil receipts has been diverted by the state oil company, the Nigerian National Petroleum Corporation (NNPC). He later reassessed the amount missing to $20 billion and called for an investigation after informing the presidency. However, political pressure from the Jonathan administration led to the resignation of the Central Bank Governor and he consequently became the traditional leader of the historic city of Kano.

Professor Okechukwu Oko provides three reasons why corruption thrives in Nigeria:[42]

1. Corrupt leadership is clearly lacking the desire and ability to change the moral tone of the country;
2. Government domination of the economic sphere significantly enhances opportunities and ability to seek rents;[43] and
3. Civil society accepts or tolerates corruption.

Professor Oko summarizes the overall effect of corruption on the political economy of Nigeria as follows:

> Official corruption possesses such corrosive potential that, if unchecked, it ultimately will destroy Nigeria. Corruption retards economic growth, distorts economic and political programs, undermines efforts to create viable economic and political institutions, devalues the quality of life, discourages foreign investment, and undermines the prospects of a durable social order in Nigeria.[44]

Overall, since independence in 1960, Nigeria has had mixed economic growth performance. The mean growth rate over the sample period 1960–2000 was −0.93 percent. During this period of forty years, there were positive growth rates in GDP per capita in nineteen years and negative growth rates in twenty-one. The highest rate of growth was 19 percent in 1969, while the lowest rate was –22.6 percent in 1975.[45] Other high negative growth rates were −21.7 percent in 2000, −19.5 percent in 1967, and −13.7 percent in 1999. Moreover, since the beginning of Nigeria's new democracy in 1999, economic performance has not improved significantly. According to the World Bank, 70 percent of Nigerians live below a poverty level of one dollar a day. Furthermore, after two years of the current political dispensation, economic stagnation was estimated at 2.8 percent in 2000, and the rate of economic growth has continued to fall below the 3 percent annual rate of population growth.[46]

GOVERNMENT SIZE, POLITICAL FREEDOM, AND ECONOMIC GROWTH: THE EMPIRICAL EVIDENCE

The two previous sections presented a historical analysis of the political economy of Nigeria since independence. In this section, an assessment of the impact of government size and political freedom on economic growth is presented. The results of the estimated impact are presented in appendix B.

Among the rankings for the degree of freedom, the impact of the rank of NF is negative and statistically significant. This negative impact shows that the rate of economic growth was lower when the country was ranked as "not free" than when it was ranked as "partly free" or "free." The rate of economic growth when the country was "not free" declined at five times the rate of growth as when the country was "free."[47] (See appendix B.) Similarly, the impact of the ranking for "free" is negative and not significantly different from zero, indicating that there is no significant difference in economic growth during periods when the country was free and periods when it was partly free. During the sample period of forty-one years, the country was rated as free in only four of those years. Thus, it appears that the number of years the country was rated as free is too limited to have had any significant impact on economic growth, as well as to distinguish its impact from that of the period in which the country was rated as partly free.[48]

The estimated impact of the size of government is negative and significant in all of the equations. These results indicate that growth in the size of government has led to a slowdown in economic growth in Nigeria. The implication of government consumption expenditure as a share of GDP, the measure of government size, is that increases in the costs of public programs do not increase the productive capacity of the economy and in fact may reduce it as found in the study. This measure of government size further indicates the extent to which government harms the economy through its spending on less productive activities and its promotion of social conflicts in the allocation of spoils.[49] According to economic theory, government's taxing and spending policies tend to create distortions in the economy, thereby leading to a slowdown in economic growth.

A related issue is whether there are differential effects of the impact of government size on economic growth among the three levels of political freedom. That is, what is the impact of government size on economic growth given that the country is free, partly free, or not free?[50] The results show that there is not a significant difference in the impact of government size on economic growth when the country is free and when it is partly free. However, the negative impact of the growth in government size on economic growth when the country is not "free" is highly significant. Overall, the impacts of government size given the various degrees of political freedom are presented in table 5.1. While growth in the size of government depresses economic growth, the negative impact of government on economic growth is much greater when the country is not free than when the country is "free" or "partly free." More political freedom tends to reduce the adverse impact of government size on the economy.

Concomitant with economic freedom is political freedom. Freedom House has classified the Nigerian economy as a mixed economic system, placing it between socialist and capitalist economic systems.[51] Government has a lesser role in economic activities in a mixed economic system than in a socialist economic system, but has a greater role than in a capitalist economic system. Societies enjoying economic freedom will tend to protect such freedom by seeking political freedom in order to control the growth and adverse effect of government on the economy. Thus, historically, democracies tend to grow out of free market economies. Democratic institutions serve as a check on the adverse effects of government on economic growth. As John Mbaku notes, "the first step toward building a sustainable economy is to adopt a constitutional democracy that safeguards economic freedom."[52] (See table 5.1.)

Table 5.1 The Impacts of Government Size and Openness of the Economy on Economic Growth Given Various Degrees of Political Freedom

	Degree of Political Freedom (%)		
	Free	*Partly Free*	*Not Free*
Variable			
Government size	0.232	−0.217	−0.274
Openness of economy	0.341	0.335	0.310

Note: These coefficients can also be interpreted as elasticities.

The impact of the openness of the economy, which shows the degree to which the country is involved in international economic transactions, is positive and highly significant. Involvement in international trade has contributed to the growth of the Nigerian economy. Virtually all developing economies are open economies (i.e., they depend significantly on international trade). As in the case of government size, a related issue is whether there is a difference in the impact of openness of the economy on economic growth when the country is free, partly free, or not free. To address this issue, the interactions between openness of the economy and the various levels of political freedom were tested.[53] The results show that there is not a statistically significant difference in the impact of openness of the economy on economic growth when the country is free and when it is partly free. However, the impact of openness is negative and statistically significant when the country is not free, indicating that the positive impact of openness of the economy on economic growth is lower when the country is not politically "free" than when the country is "free." Thus, less political freedom in the country reduces the benefits of international economic transactions. Using the point estimates as elasticity's, the impacts of openness of the economy are reported in table 5.1.[54] Promoting civil and political liberties and openness of the economy appear to be important determinants of economic growth. As many studies have concluded, open economies grow more rapidly than closed economies.[55]

The impact of two main factors of production, investment as a share of GDP and growth of population as a proxy for the labor force, is statistically significant. Population growth has a positive effect, indicating that it promotes economic growth. On the other hand, investment as a share of GDP is negatively related to economic growth in Nigeria. (See appendix B.)

An analysis of the components of total investment in Nigeria reveals why investment has a negative impact on economic growth. Total investment consists of public investment and private investment. The basic rational for public investment by government is that private firms and households will not undertake certain investment, such as building roads and bridges, because of externality. However, this does not mean that all public sector infrastructure investments are worthwhile. For example, governments have been known to build fancy superhighways connecting the capital city to the president's village or large showcase dam projects that never pay for themselves.[56] In the case of Nigeria, the political and military elites implemented public projects that proved to be money-draining projects. For example, the Ajaokuta Steel Plant that cost over US$6 billion is yet to produce any steel.[57] In the 1990s, the proposed hydroelectric dam for Zungeru and the Oji coal-powered stations, estimated at 1.2 billion dollars, was more expensive than equivalent gas turbines.[58] Government contracts were also awarded at inflated prices by as much as three or four times their worth, and development projects were shoddily executed or completely abandoned after mobilization fees had been paid. In other instances there was looting of public funds necessary for savings and investment. For example, about 60 percent of every dollar of oil revenue earned during the 1980s and $1.5 billion of the proceeds from petroleum exports in 1990 were unaccounted for.[59] By 1991, $1 billion had been spent for undocumented purposes out of the 2 billion dollars that Nigeria realized from the sale of its equity in a joint venture with Shell Oil Company.[60] These examples indicate that public investment may not have contributed to economic growth in Nigeria.

Private investment, the other component of total investment, provides the thrust for growth. In most developing countries, the private sector is the main channel for investment.[61] A source of investment funds is gross national savings, which consists of domestic and foreign savings. Gross national savings as a percentage of gross national income declined from 18.6 percent in 1975 to 16.5 in 1994 in Nigeria. Domestic savings consist primarily of government and private domestic savings. Given the low per capita income in Nigeria, as in other low-income developing countries, the household component of private domestic savings may be low and thus may not be a major source of investment. With respect to government savings, it has declined significantly. As a percent of gross domestic national income, government savings declined from 4.2 percent in 1975 to −2.0 percent in 1994.[62] Thus, savings have not been a major source of investment funds and hence economic growth in Nigeria.

Frequent regime changes have also contributed to lower private investment in Nigeria. During its forty-five years of independence (1960–2005), the country has experienced more than six coups d'état, twenty-nine years of military rule, and only sixteen years of civilian rule. Such frequent regime changes, concomitant with policy uncertainties, have led to lower long-run investment and output in Nigeria, as well as other African countries.[63]

Moreover, private investment also has been deterred by public and private corrupt practices, such as "advance fee" fraudsters or "419" scams. The term "four-one-nine" is coined after Section 419 of the Nigerian Criminal Code, which stipulates that "where a person by false presence and with intent to defraud, obtains another person's property, that a felony has been committed by that person."[64] The scam is conducted mainly through an e-mail in which the e-mail recipient is requested to enter into some financial transaction with the sender or fraudster in return for a large financial reward. The fraudster usually claims to have millions of dollars that a deceased relative left for him in a bank in Nigeria or abroad or claims to have information about the records on millions of dollars left for the recipient by some deceased relative of the recipient. The recipient is asked to provide advance fees to process the necessary documents to retrieve the funds and is also asked to provide a bank account in which the funds retrieved will be deposited to be shared. The fraudster defrauds the recipient by taking the advance fees and, in some instances, by withdrawing whatever funds the recipient may have in the bank account.[65] Many people in and outside Nigeria have been victims of this scam. The scam has tarnished Nigeria's international image and has deterred potential foreign investors from investing in the country.[66] Moreover, such an illegal transaction diverts scarce resources from productive activities and reduces economic growth. Thus, on the average, investment has not had a positive impact on economic growth in Nigeria.

This finding is consistent with the conclusions of a recent study that "there is no association between increases in investment in Africa and changes in growth from 1960 to 1999."[67] In that study, Shantayanan Devarajan, William Easterly, and Howard Pack found that public and private investments are not correlated with growth in Africa except in the case of Botswana, the only country to have experienced high private investment rates and high growth. Botswana's success can be attributed to several policies, such as budget surplus, political stability, and democratic governance, which tend to be lacking in many African countries including Nigeria.[68] This has led to lower long-run investment and output in many of these countries such as Nigeria.[69] Thus, the lack of association between investment and economic growth in Africa found in that study and the negative association between investment and economic growth in Nigeria found in our study indicate that investment has not promoted economic growth in Nigeria.

SUMMARY

The impacts of government size, the degree of political freedom, and the degree of openness of the economy on economic growth has been assessed in the case of Nigeria using an adaptation of a neoclassical growth model. Growth in government size was found to depress economic growth. The impact of government size on the economy varies among various degrees of political freedom, with the negative impact being greater when the country is not "free" than when the country is "free" or "partly free." Government seems to create distortions in the economy through its taxing and spending policies. However, the impact of these distortions on economic growth is less when the country is politically free than when it is not.

The degree of openness of the economy was also an important determinant of economic growth. The more involved the country is in international economic transactions, the higher the rate of economic growth. However, less political freedom depresses the benefits of openness of the economy.

Overall, political freedom appears to be an important determinant of economic growth in Nigeria. Political freedom not only promotes economic growth, but it also reduces the negative impact of government on the economy and enhances the benefits from international economic transactions. Thus, the adoption of a politically free institutional framework that protects economic freedom is an important condition for promoting economic growth.

NOTES

1. Wale Olaitan, "The State and Economy in Nigeria: A Conceptualization," in Said Adejumobi and Momoh Abubakar (eds.), *The Political Economy of Nigeria Under the Military Rule: 1984–1993* (Harare, Zimbabwe: SAPES Books, 1995).
2. Ibid.
3. Robin Luckham, *The Nigerian Military: A Sociological Analysis of Authority and Revolt* (Cambridge, UK: Cambridge University, 1971).
4. Ibid.
5. Oladimeji Aborisade and Robert J. Mundt, *Politics in Nigeria* (New York: Longman Publishers, 2002).
6. Ethnologists have identified over 250 ethnic groups in Nigeria. However, there are three major ethnic groups: Hausa-Fulani from the North, Igbo from the Southeast, and Yoruba from the Southwest.
7. Aborisade and Mundt, *Politics in Nigeria,* 18–19.
8. Fredoline O. Anunobi, *The Implications of Conditionality: The International Monetary Fund and Africa* (Landham, MD: University Press of America, 1992).
9. Adebayo Olukoshi, *The Politics of Structural Adjustment in Nigeria* (Ibadan: Heinemann Educational Books, 1993).
10. Adebayo Olukoshi, "The Political Economy of the Structural Adjustment Program," in Said Adejumobi and Momoh Abubakar (ed.), *The Political Economy of Nigeria Under the Military Rule: 1984–1993* (Harare, Zimbabwe: SAPES Books, 1995), 139.
11. Ibid.
12. Ibid.
13. Ibid.
14. Ibid.: In September 1986, the Babangida administration introduced a two-tier exchange market. The first tier foreign exchange market was used to service external

debt and other official transfers to international organizations. The second-tier foreign exchange market is the market where the Naira was allowed to depreciate on the basis of bids submitted by local banks purchasing foreign exchange from the Nigerian Central Bank.

15. Aborisade and Mundt, *Politics in Nigeria.*

16. Ibid.

17. Ibid.

18. Sani Abacha, "Domestic Policy," *Nigerian Economist* 7, no. 31 (May 2, 1994), 4.

19. Eme Amuzie, Gofrey Ikhemuemhe, and Martins Azukiwe, "No Way Out," *Nigerian Economist* 7, no. 31 (May 2, 1994), 12.

20. Richard Sklar, Ebere Onwudiwe, and Darren Kew, "Nigeria: Completing Obasanjo's Legacy," *Journal of Democracy* 17, no. 3 (2006), 100–15.

21. Richard Skylar, Beer Onwudiwe, and Darren Kew, "Nigeria: Completing Obasanjo's Legacy."

22. "No Third Term Bid for Nigeria Leader." http://news.bbc.co.uk/2/hi/africa/.

23. Ibid.

24. "Country Brief on Nigeria," *CIA Fact Book.* https://www.cia.gov/library/publications/the-world-factbook/geos/ni.html#top.

25. A. J. Omede "Nigerian: Analyzing the Security Challenges of the Goodluck Jonathan Administration," *Canadian Social Science* 7, no. 5 (2011), 90–102.

26. Ibid., 90.

27. Mohammed H.A Bolaji, "Between Democracy and Federalism: Shariah in Northern Nigeria and the Paradox of Institutional Impetuses," *Africa Today* 59, no. 4 (2013), 3–117.

28. John Campbell, "Nigeria's Battle for Stability," *National Interest* 118 (2012), 36.

29. Wole Soyinka, "'Baptism By Fire': *Boko Haram and the Reign of in Nigeria,*" ed. Benjamin Maiangwa, Ufo Okeke Uzodike, Ayo Whetho, and Hakeem Onapajo: 59, no. 2 (2012), 41–57.

30. "BBC Nigerian Election. Muhammadu Buhari Wins Presidency." http://www.bbc.com//news/world-affairs-32139858.

31. "Why Buhari Axed Service Chiefs Ahead of US Visit," *Vanguard Newspaper.* file:///Users/user/Desktop/Why%20Buhari%20axed%20Service%20Chiefs%20ahead%20of%20US%20visit!%20-%20Vanguard%20News.html.

32. Pete Hoekstra, "Buhari is Nigeria's Problem, Not its Solution: It's Hard to See How President Buhari's Policies Are Good for the Future," *World Street Journal.* June 16, 2016. https://www.wsj.com/articles/buhari-is-nigerias-problem-not-its-solution-1466109183.

33. Ibid.

34. "Nigerian Economy Stats," Nationmaster.com. http://www.nationmaster.com/country-info/profiles/Nigeria/Economy.

35. Madu Onuroah, "Government Spends N92 Billion on Debt Servicing in 10 Months," *Guardian Newspaper,* 2003. http//www.odili.net; Retrieved October 13, 2003. Izevbuwa Osayimwese and Sunday Iyare, "The Economics of Nigerian

Federalism: Selected Issues in Economic Management," *Publius: The Journal of Federalism* 21 (Fall 1991), 89–101.

36. Adetutu Folasade-Koyi, "Public Enterprises Indicted in N3.8 Trillion Debt," *Daily Independent*, May 10, 2003. http://www.odili.net.

37. Cheryl Prayer, "Causes of the Debt Crisis," in Bade Onimade (ed.), *The IMF, The World Bank, and the African Debt: The Economic Impact* (London: Zed Books, 1989).

38. Alan Heston and Robert Summers, "Penn World Tables at Chass: Computing in the Humanities and Social Sciences." http://datacentre2.chass.uronto.cal/pwt/; The data was for the year 1998.

39. Transparency International, "Global Regional and Country Reports." http://www.transparency.org/cpi2014/results.

40. Ibid.

41. Ibid.

42. Okechukwu Oko, "Subverting the Source of Corruption in Nigeria: A Reform Prospectus," *New York University Journal of International Law & Politics* 34 (2002), 397–474.

43. With respect to this reason Professor Oko provides for the pervasiveness of corruption in Nigeria, one can argue that there are some countries, such as Denmark, Norway, and Sweden, in which government involvement in the economy has not necessarily led to corruption. It appears that weak political institutions in Nigeria explain why corruption thrives in Nigeria. See the section in this chapter entitled "Assessing Nigerian Political Economy" for our discussion of the impact of Nigeria's weak political institutions on economic growth.

44. Okechukwu Oko, "Subverting the Source of Corruption in Nigeria."

45. It is interesting to note that the highest and lowest growth rates of per capita income occurred during the military regime of General Yakubu Gowon (1966–1975), who came to power through a military coup in 1966.The Gowon administration had established a wage commission (The Udoji Commission) in 1974 to restructure civil service wages especially for the upper-scale of the civil service. This might have shored-up per capita income, since the civil service in Nigeria is the largest employer of labor. The restructuring of the civil service wages was made possible by the windfall from oil prices of 1974. See also Dafe Otobo, "Bureaucratic Elites and Public Sector Wage Bargaining in Nigeria," *Journal of Modern African Studies* 24 (1986), 110–26.

46. Rotimi Suberu, "Can Nigeria's New Democracy Survive," *Current History* (2001), 207–12. At the same time, the national currency depreciated in value from 90 naira to a dollar in early 1999, to 125 naira by early 2001 and to nearly 129 naira in 2003.

47. Although the variables were not significant, the point estimates were used.

48. During the forty-one-year sample period, Nigeria is rated "partly free" for twenty-two years and as "not free" for fifteen years.

49. J. Hirshleifer, "The Paradox of Power," *Economics and Politics* 3 (1991), 177–200.

50. To address this issue, the interactions between government size and the various degrees of political freedom are tested (see appendix B, equation 2). The impact

of government size on economic growth for a given level of political freedom is the sum of the coefficient of the additive term of the government size variable and the coefficient of the relevant interaction variable. The point estimates are also used as elasticities.

51. Raymond Gastil, *Freedom in the World* (West Port: Greenwood, 1986); "The New Criteria of Freedom," *Freedom at Issue* 17 (1973), 2–23.

52. John Mukum Mbaku, "Entrenching Economic Freedom in Africa," *The Cato Journal* 23, no. 2 (2003), 217–25.

53. See appendix B, equation 3. The impact of openness on economic growth for a given level of political freedom is obtained by adding the coefficient of the additive term of the variable for openness and the coefficient of the respective interaction variable.

54. Ibid.

55. James S. Guseh, "Government Size and Economic Growth in Developing Countries: A Political-Economy Framework," *Journal of Macroeconomics* 19, no. 1 (1997), 175–92; Jean-Paul Azam, Augustin Fosu, and Njuguna S. Ndung'u, "Explaining Slow Growth in Africa," *African Development Bank* (Malden, MA: Blackwell Publishers, 2002), citing W. Easterly, "The Joys and Sorrows of Openness: A Review Essay," forthcoming as a book by Kluwer Academic Publishers.

56. Dwight H. Perkins, Steven Radelet, Donald R. Snodgrass, Malcolm Gillis, and Michael Roemer, *Economics of Development*, Fifth edition (New York: W.W. Norton & Company, 2001), 312.

57. Onuorah, "Government Spends N92 billion on Debt Servicing in 10 Months,"; Osayimwese and Iyare, "The Economics of Nigerian Federalism: Selected Issues in Economic Management," 89–101.

58. Dulue Nbuchu, "The Looting of Nigeria," *African Guardian* (November 1, 1993), 2.

59. Ibid.

60. Ibid.

61. Perkins, Radeler, Snodgrass, Gillis, and Roemer, *Economics of Development*, 384.

62. Ibid., 394.

63. Byeongju Jeong. "Policy Uncertainty and Long-run Investment and Output Across Countries," *International Economic Review* 43, no. 2 (2002), 363–92.

64. Ichechukwu. Agwa, "Legal Opinion on Section 419 Criminal Code Laws of Nigeria," (Lagos, Nigeria: Rhodes & Rhodes, Barristers, Solicitors & Notaries Public [2004]). Unpublished.

65. Thompson, Nicolas, "You've Got Fraud," *Foreign Policy* (May/June2003), 1–2.

66. Caspar Fithin, "Nigeria-Rapacious Corruption," *Oxford Analytical Weekly* (September 27, 2000), column, 1–4.

67. Shantayanan Devarajan, William Easterly, and Howard Pack. "Low Investment is Not the Constraint on African Development," *Economic Development and Cultural Change* 70 (2003), 547–71.

68. Ibid., 556.

69. Jeong, "Policy Uncertainty and Long-run Investment and Output Across Countries."

Chapter 6

The African Growth and Opportunity Act and Economic Growth in Africa

Since the 1960s and 1970s, when most SSA countries gained independence from colonial rule, achieving economic growth and development has been a central objective of governments in the region, as well as international donor organizations. The Organization of African Unity—now the African Union—was established to promote development at the economic, social, and cultural levels, and to foster the integration of African economies,[1] among others. In order to address specific regional concerns, organizations such as the ECOWAS, East African Community, and Southern African Development Community, were also established. At the same time, several international organizations, including the United Nations, African Development Bank, World Bank, and IMF, have expressed their commitment to improving economic conditions in SSA by providing billions of dollars' worth of funding and various forms of policy consultation. Governments of developed and industrialized countries have also provided substantial forms of development assistance through foreign aid. The ultimate objective of this assistance is to transition African countries from that state of poverty to integration in the global economic community.

Despite the substantial resources and numerous policy prescriptions for the development of SSA, success has been scattered and slow. When African countries gained political independence, they did not achieve economic independence. As Upsall (2013) asserts, while political independence can occur with the sweep of a pen and a handshake at a ceremony, where economic independence does not occur concurrently. Economic independence by nature takes a longer period of time to establish, especially for the newly independent states to transition from the colonial system to the global economic system. Massive foreign aid was provided in the SSA region with the hope of accelerating the process. The foreign aid for nearly six decades, however, has not produced a sustainable economic improvement in many SSA countries. Yet funds continue to flow into Africa with little to show. In 2009, Moyo found this perpetuation of the aid culture as the single most important aspect keeping African states from succeeding in economic development.[2] For example, one of the widely known policies that failed to address Africa's problem of economic growth and development was the World Bank's SAP in the 1980s, aimed at privatization and free markets; unfortunately, these reform programs failed to achieve the intended objectives. Loans from multilateral institutions (e.g. the IMF and the World Bank) and assistance from other international donor organizations and governments have not led to sustainable growth and development.

Proponents of aid, however, use the US Marshall Plan at the end of World War II as an example of how development aid can rebuild a state and establish a strong engine for participation in the global market economic system. The Marshall Plan (officially the European Recovery Program [ERP]) was an American initiative to aid Western Europe, in which the United States gave over $12 billion (approximately $120 billion in current dollar value as of June 2016) in economic support to help rebuild Western European economies after the end of World War II. The aid initially resulted in shipments of food, staples, fuel, and machinery from the United States and later resulted in investment in industrial capacity in Europe. The aid also included administrative and technical assistance provided through the Economic Cooperation Administration of the United States. Marshall Plan nations were assisted greatly in their economic recovery. From 1948 to 1952, European economies grew at an unprecedented rate. Trade relations led to the formation of the North Atlantic Alliance. Economic prosperity led by coal and steel industries helped to shape what is now known as the EU.

In distinguishing the structure of the Marshall Plan from the foreign aid to Africa, Moyo states that the Marshall Plan was much better designed and executed when compared to African developmental aid. The Marshall Plan was implemented for a period of time and also provided a short period of funding. Much of Africa has received aid continually for at least fifty years.[3] The Marshall Plan had a stated quantifiable goal of rebuilding European infrastructure and infusing capital into a broken economic system. African development aid has been propping up a broken system and perpetuating colonial habits of weak state governments and economies based on a system that does not foster the growth of the state. Most colonial possessions were created with the purpose of settlement or resource extraction. Once the political independence of colonial states was granted, the economy of the former colonized states was still structured on resource extraction. While political independence was realized, the economies still maintained the colonial economic structure based on resource extraction. Thus, only a few independent states were prepared to transition from colonial economic system to global capitalist system.

Moreover, problems in realizing long-term economic growth and development in the region can be attributed to corruption and plunder of state resources by African leaders and bureaucrats,[4] the general paucity of investment resources,[5] the debt crisis, the lack of political stability,[6] weak governance institutions, and the HIV/AIDS pandemic.[7] According to the World Bank, gross domestic investment accounted for only 17.9 percent of GDP in 2000, while FDI in Africa declined from approximately 25 percent to 5 percent in 2003.[8] Additionally, the debt burden of most SSA countries has been a major factor in the economic decline of the continent as a whole. At the end of 2002 SSA countries alone owed foreign creditors $208.9 billion.[9] The HIV/AIDS pandemic also presents enormous social and economic development challenges. The incidence rate of HIV/AIDS in SSA is 8.4 percent, the highest in the world.[10] The impact of the disease on the most productive members of the society—rural farmers, skilled workers, teachers, and other professionals—will adversely affect the productive capacity of the economies in the region. The vulnerability of SSA to infectious diseases, such as HIV/AIDS, tuberculosis, and malaria, is further compounded by poverty. Nearly half of the people in SSA live on less than a dollar a day, and with a dearth of social infrastructures, such as health care facilities and education, HIV/AIDS-related mortality rates are likely to soar.[11] Furthermore, SSA countries continue to face massive development challenges, such as military intervention in national politics, competition for participation in political and economic markets, dependence on the industrial market economies of the West for trade and loans.

Given these economic and political problems, it is widely accepted that the future development of SSA will depend to a large extent on good governance and the success of individual economies in attracting FDI for growth sectors,[12] as well as participation in regional and international trade. It is against this background that the administration of United States President, William Jefferson Clinton, decided to promote in Africa the same prescription that the United States had employed in European countries. This paradigm is based on the principle that the United States has profound interests in prosperity and peace worldwide, and open trade helps to achieve these objectives. Therefore, US trade policy toward Africa must be shaped by the same principles as its policy toward other regions of the world. Concessions in the area of trade provide better long-term prospects for developing countries' economic development than do concessions in aid.[13] If Africa is to develop and prosper, the region must be open to trade and investment with the United States, its regional neighbors,[14] and the rest of the world. Such openness will lead to growth, competition, and broad-based prosperity. Thus, in 2000 the Clinton administration launched the AGOA with the aim of eliminating trade barriers in order to increase FDI and gain market share in the industrial supplier sector of SSA economy.[15] Since then, three other presidential administrations—George Bush, Barrack Obama, and Donald Trump—have dealt with AGOA.

THE WILLIAM CLINTON ADMINISTRATION AND AGOA

In the 1990s the Clinton administration sought a stable, economically dynamic, and democratic Africa. The way in which the administration sought to achieve these goals was through US trade partnerships with African countries. As stated by Witney Schneidman, Deputy Assistant Secretary of State for African Affairs during the Clinton era:

> The Clinton administration has made it a priority of its foreign policy to support increased economic growth in Africa in order to accelerate the region's integration into the global economy through trade and investment. We believe that trade and investment is critical to Africa's long-term sustained development.[16]

In June 1997, the Clinton administration unveiled the Partnership for Economic Growth and Opportunity in Africa. The centerpiece of this program was the AGOA, which was signed into US law on May 18, 2000, as Title 1 of the US Trade and Development Act of 2000. This policy initiative was aimed at eliminating trade barriers in order to increase FDI and gain market share in the industrial supplier sector of the SSA economy.[17] The focus of the administration's policy under AGOA is spelled out in the following broadly stated objectives:

1. Strengthening and expanding the private sector in SSA, especially women-owned businesses;
2. Encouraging increased trade and investment between the United States and SSA;
3. Reducing tariff and non-tariff barriers and other trade obstacles;
4. Expanding US assistance to SSA's regional integration efforts;
5. Establishing a US and SSA Trade and Investment Partnership;
6. Focusing on countries committed to accountable government including continual progress toward establishing political pluralism, and rule of law, economic reform, and the eradication of poverty;
7. Establishing a US–sub-Saharan Economic Cooperation Forum; and
8. Supporting development assistance for those countries in SSA that are attempting to build civil societies.[18]

By way of summary, the Act authorizes the president to designate countries as eligible to receive benefits of AGOA if they are determined to have established or are making continual progress toward the following:

> The Act authorizes the President to designate countries as eligible to receive the benefits of AGOA if they are determined to have established, or are making continual progress toward establishing the following: market-based economies; the rule of law and political pluralism; elimination of barriers to US trade and investment; protection of intellectual property; efforts to combat corruption; policies to reduce poverty, increasing availability of health care and educational opportunities; protection of human rights and worker rights; and elimination of certain child labor practices. These criteria have been embraced overwhelmingly by the vast majority of African nations, which are striving to achieve the objectives although none is expected to have fully implemented the entire list.[19]

The AGOA was also intended to be a major departure from the benefits that SSA's exports had attained under the Generalized System of Preferences (GSP). It is useful for the purpose of this study to examine the extent to which AGOA has led to changes in trade policies between United States and SSA countries when compared to the effect of GSP on these policies.

GSP is a program designed to promote economic growth in the developing world by providing preferential, duty-free entry for more than 4650 products from 144 designated beneficiary countries and territories.[20] The program, which was authorized under the Trade Act of 1974 for a ten-year period, was instituted on January 1, 1976. It has been renewed periodically since then, most recently in 2002, when President George W. Bush signed legislation that reauthorized it through 2006. Under the GSP system forty-eight SSA countries were granted preferential access to the US market, and were expected to pay zero tariffs, but were subject to certain conditions for a range of exports under GSP. In 2000 the program covered about $4 billion of Africa's total exports of $23 billion. The margin of preference for SSA when compared with other Most Favored Nation (MFN) countries was estimated at 5 percent.[21] The AGOA has seen a change in policy direction from the GSP system in three major ways:

1. The existing preferential access that SSA countries enjoyed under the GSP system was extended in time.
2. AGOA also increased the range of products in which preferential access was granted. For instance, petroleum, apparels, and agricultural and industrial products were further granted preferential access.[22]
3. Only two SSA countries, Mauritius and Kenya, faced quotas, with Mauritius being subject to quotas as high as 25 percent on its exports.

The eligibility criteria for GSP and AGOA substantially overlap, and countries must be GSP eligible in order to receive AGOA's trade benefits, including both expanded GSP and the apparel provisions. Although GSP eligibility does not imply AGOA eligibility, forty-seven of the forty-eight countries in SSA were GSP eligible.

The benefits of AGOA for SSA countries will be driven by compliance with the rules of origin under the GSP system. These rules are typified under two broad categories: rules of origin for non-apparel exports and rules of origin for apparel exports. Under the first category, exporting countries of non-apparel products that are eligible for duty-free access under AGOA can meet the 35 percent value-added content by counting production or materials from other beneficiary countries and the United States.[23] Under the second category, AGOA requires that apparel be assembled in eligible SSA countries and that the yarn and fabric be made in the United States or in an African country. Guidelines also state that this rule would not be applicable to the least developed countries until 2004. Furthermore, it instituted a cap of 1.5 percent of all US imports, which was expected to grow to 3.5 percent of all imports over an eight-year period.[24] The October 2000 version of AGOA (AGOA I) conferred quota- and duty-free status to clothing articles directly imported into the United States from beneficiary countries until September 30, 2008.[25] To command beneficiary status, countries had to meet a series of political and economic conditions, which resulted in thirty-eight countries having beneficiary status.

AGOA distinguishes between a lesser developed beneficiary country (LDBC) and other African countries with regard to clothing rules of origin. The Act defines LDBC as countries with a per capita gross national product of less than $1,500 in 1998 as measured by the World Bank. The term, "Former Beneficiary SSA Country," means that after being designated as a beneficiary country, the country ceased to be designated as such by reason of its entering into a free trade agreement with the United States. An eligible country is one that is an eligible SSA country under AGOA.[26]

At least until September 30, 2004, LDBCs had preferential access on the basis of a single-stage rule, meaning that only assembly and finishing of products in the country of origin was required. Non-LDBCs, such as Mauritius and South Africa, enjoy the same access on the basis of a three-stage rule. The three-stage rule states the following: (1) yarn spinning, (2) fabric weaving or knitting, and (3) assembly and finishing must take place in the country of origin, another beneficiary country or the United States. A cap of 3.5 percent by volume was applied to all US imports benefiting from AGOA preferences.[27] (See appendix C for a summary of the apparel rules of origin under AGOA.)

President Clinton issued a proclamation on October 2, 2000, designating thirty-four countries in SSA as eligible for the trade benefits of AGOA.

The proclamation was the result of opinions and suggestions offered during a public-comment period and extensive interagency deliberations of each country's performance against the eligibility criteria established in the Act.[28]

THE GEORGE W. BUSH ADMINISTRATION

The Bush administration's policy on AGOA did not shift much from the original theme of AGOA. Beneficiary countries must continue to show commitment to building democratic market institutions, human rights, and good governance in return for the expanded trade with the United States. Concessions in trade and investment, it is believed, provide better prospects for economic prosperity than do the ones in aid. As stated by US Congressman Ed Royce, by increasing trade with African countries the United States will increase the institutional building capacity of SSA governments and improve the standard of living for Africans. Such a relationship between the United States and SSA countries will create an environment in which people can exercise their freedom and liberties, as well as an environment in which terrorists cannot thrive—a major concern of the United States.[29]

The Bush administration provided two amendments to AGOA, known as AGOA II and AGOA III. AGOA II, also known as the Trade Act of 2002, was signed by President Bush on August 6, 2002, and became effective immediately. It was designed to improve the operation of AGOA I and improve SSA countries' utilization of the AGOA program. AGOA II clarifies and narrowly expands the trade opportunities for SSA countries and encourages more investment in the region. AGOA II also proposed to increase the cap to 7 percent of all US imports benefiting from AGOA preferences and resolved problems of eligibility for certain knitwear and merino wool articles.[30] Finally, it provided additional congressional guidance to the executive branch on how to administer the textile provisions of the bill.

Although President Bush initially maintained the thirty-four SSA countries that had previously been declared AGOA eligible under the Clinton administration, he later removed some of these countries that he declared ineligible and added other countries he declared eligible,[31] bringing the total number of AGOA eligible countries to forty-one. The United States government was to work with eligible countries to institute policy reforms and also to help the remaining eight SSA countries achieve eligibility.[32] The list of AGOA-eligible countries is presented in appendix D.

The second amendment to AGOA (AGOA III), also known as the Acceleration Act of 2004, was signed by President Bush on July 12, 2004. AGOA III, which was intended to strengthen AGOA I, approved the designation of thirty-seven SSA countries as eligible for tariff preferences under AGOA.

However, President Bush removed the Central African Republic and Eritrea from the list of beneficiary countries to the list of former beneficiary countries and accorded Angola an eligible beneficiary status.[33] AGOA III also provided the following:

1. Extended preferential access for imports from beneficiary SSA countries until September 30, 2015;
2. Extended third-country fabric provision for three years, from September 2004 until September 2007; and
3. Provided additional congressional guidance to the executive on how to administer the textile provisions of the bill.

The thrust of the Bush administration policy objectives toward Africa was driven by three factors. First, there was a departure from the Clinton administration's reliance on regional leaders to ensure regional stability. Instead, the Bush administration emphasized a long-term approach that would focus on true regional powers that combine both economic and military capabilities. Second, the Bush administration intended to build upon the Clinton administration's success in promoting US trade and investment with African countries as a reward for developing liberal, free market economies. This approach would serve as the basis for strengthening the AGOA. The third and final aspect of the Bush administration policy toward Africa, which is also consistent with the Clinton administration approach, is the view that African countries must become self-reliant and less dependent.

On December 20, 2006, President Bush signed another amendment to AGOA, known as the African Investment Incentive Act of 2006. This legislation, referred to as AGOA IV, extended textile and apparel provisions of the AGOA program until 2015. It also extended the third-country fabric provision until 2012, and increased the cap to 3.5 percent beginning October 1, 2006.

THE BARACK OBAMA ADMINISTRATION

The AGOA, signed by President Bill Clinton in 2000, allow several dozen SSA countries to export to the US duty-free. The program was set to expire in 2015. Barack Obama came to the White House promising to "strengthen the African Growth and Opportunity Act to ensure that African producers can access the US market and will encourage more American companies to invest on the continent."

Upon assuming office as President of the United States, Barrack Obama did not define his policy on AGOA. However, during his campaign for president in 2008, one of Obama's foreign policy advisers, Director Witney Schneidman, listed three fundamental objectives that Obama would pursue in Africa, some of which are consistent with the objectives of AGOA: (1) "accelerate Africa's integration into the global economy"; (2) "enhance the peace and security of African states"; and (3) "strengthen relationships with those governments, institutions, and civil society organizations committed to deepening democracy, accountability, and reducing poverty in Africa."[34]

African governments and the business community believed that Obama's ascension would open doors and opportunities for Africa. For instance, Kenya expected President Obama's administration to support the current trade arrangements under AGOA. At the Seventh AGOA Forum held July 14 to 16, 2008 in Washington, DC, Kenya's Deputy Prime Minister, Uhuru Kenyatta, and Chair of the African Consultative Group of Ministers on AGOA, said he would work closely with the new administration to expand the trade pact for the mutual benefits of their people.[35] Ministers from AGOA-eligible countries at the Forum requested that AGOA be made permanent and predictable in order to make the region more attractive to foreign investments, especially from corporate America.

During President Obama's first time in office, the most concrete legislative action was the enactment of H.R. 5986, which included provisions affecting AGOA as well as trade with the Dominican Republic and Myanmar (formerly Burma). The bill extended provisions within AGOA that allowed African nations to import raw textiles from non-African nations, process them in Africa, and then export them to the United States duty free. This commerce totals $1.3 billion in products.[36]

When the law was written, this "third-country" provision had been scheduled to expire as the African textile industry gradually improved its infrastructure. However, the expected improvements never materialized, and policymakers realized that the sudden expiration of the "third-country" provision threatened to throw perhaps 150,000 African textile workers out of work.[37] To ameliorate this, in August 2012 the AGOA was amended to extend the third-country fabric program to 2015.

One feature of the legislation does expand AGOA, at least in a technical sense. The measure signed by Obama added South Sudan to the list of nations that qualify for trade status under AGOA. South Sudan voted for independence in 2011, meaning it did not exist as an independent state when the law was written. In addition, Obama took a number of other actions that could eventually bolster trade with Africa. In June 2011, the United States announced an African Competitiveness and Trade Expansion initiative to provide up to $120 million over four years to improve Africa's trade capacity, including products that can enter duty-free under AGOA, and in the same month, the United States proposed a new partnership with the East African community that would include a possible regional investment treaty and other trade agreements. Finally, Obama used his executive powers to designate forty SSA countries eligible for AGOA benefits in 2012.[38]

Although the Act has not been successful in all areas, it has been reported to have had a considerable impact on SSA's clothing industry and is a key part of the reason that textile plants have popped up across the region and also explains why the trousers Americans buy at Walmart are increasingly from countries such as Ghana.[39] After completing its initial year period of validity, the AGOA legislation was extended on June 29, 2015, by ten years to 2025.

The challenges to America and President Obama were many and far more complex than they had been in recent history. Obama had to turn the US economy around, end the war in Iraq while shifting focus to Afghanistan and fixing America's schools and health care system, among many other pressing issues to the American people. Balancing these needs of the United States with those of SSA countries under AGOA was one of the challenges facing the administration.

THE TRUMP ADMINISTRATION

As soon as Donald Trump became the next president of the United States, he raised alarms across Africa when he said that AGOA was benefiting corrupt regimes in Africa because, as he claimed, most imports under AGOA are petroleum products. The alarm was further exacerbated when the Trump administration declared to put the interests of the United States first, thereby creating uncertainty in world trade. However, according to the US trade representative Robert Lighthizer, the United States is determined to engage in deeper commercial trade with Africa.[40]

ASSESSMENT OF AGOA

AGOA can be assessed on several objective criteria. Overall, AGOA has had mixed results. For a country to be AGOA eligible, the country must promote political reform and political pluralism. An assessment of democratic trends in SSA shows that there have been progress and setbacks. Political instability and violent disputes about the fairness of elections have occurred in countries, such as Ivory Coast, Zimbabwe, Burundi, Southern Sudan, and Madagascar. In Gabon, given the closeness of the election results, a dispute arose when the opposition party demanded a recount. On the other hand remarkable progress has been realized in Ghana and Nigeria, where there were peaceful transitions of government, a reflection of the democratic process.

Table 6.1 Democratic Trends in Sub-Saharan Africa since the Adoption of AGOA in 2000

	Free		*Partly Free*		*Not Free*	
Survey Edition	*Number of Countries*	*Percentage*	*Number of Countries*	*Percentage*	*Number of Countries*	*Percentage*
2016	9	18	20	41	20	41
2015	10	20	18	37	21	43
2014	10	20	19	39	20	42
2013	11	22	18	37	20	41
2012	9	18	21	43	19	39
2011	9	19	22	46	17	35
2010	9	19	23	48	16	33
2009	10	21	23	48	15	31
2008	11	23	23	48	14	29
2007	11	23	22	46	15	31
2006	11	23	23	48	14	29
2005	11	23	21	44	16	33
2004	11	23	20	42	17	35
2003	11	23	21	44	16	33
2001–2002	9	19	25	52	14	29
2000–2001	9	19	24	50	15	31
1999–2000	8	17	24	50	16	33

Source: Freedom House "Democratic Trends in sub-Saharan Africa" https://freedomhouse.org/resource/democratic-trends-sub-saharan-africa Accessed June 4, 2015.

Table 6.1 shows country rankings of political freedom in SSA. As explained in chapter 1, Freedom House has provided three categories of freedom ranking for countries as "free, partly free, and not free." The table shows the trends in the rankings in the SSA region since the establishment of AGOA in 2000.

In the year AGOA was adopted, nine countries were ranked as free, and in 2016 the number increased to 19 percent. Over the same period the number ranked as partly free decline from 21 to 20, respectively, and the not free countries increased from 16 to 20. In terms of percentages over the same period, the partly free countries declined slightly from 19 percent to 18 percent, the partly free declined from 50 to 41 percent, and the not free increased significantly from 31 to 41 percent. Since the adoption of AGOA political freedom or democracy in SSA has not improved or has improved marginally. Similar findings are found in North Africa. Although one of the objectives of AGOA was designed for African countries to promote democratic market institutions, progress has been slowed down. While progress is being made in some countries, there are setbacks in others.

On the economic front AGOA is making important contribution in trade. Appendix E presents the total monetary values of exports, imports, and the trade balances between the United States and AGOA beneficiary countries from 2000, when AGOA was adopted, to 2015. Since the adoption of AGOA, the United States has had a negative trade balance with SSA, indicating that the United States is importing more goods from Africa than it is exporting to the region. The combined values of the exports of AGOA countries to the United States have consistently exceeded the combined values of their imports from the United States, indicating a positive trade balance in favor of the AGOA countries. African countries are therefore benefiting from trade with the United States.

The passage of the Act represented a shift from previous US trade policy toward Africa, which typically focused on aid instead of trade. This shift in policy is influenced by the neoclassical paradigm that economic growth should be promoted through trade and investment, as well as the emergent economic dynamism that SSA countries appeared to have realized in the late 1990s and early 2000s.[41] Akech contends, these factors along with the realization of the size of the African market prompted the Clinton administration to pursue trade partnership with SSA.[42]

AGOA provides unrestricted access to exports of a wide range of products, such as energy and related products, agricultural products, and minerals to US markets.[43] Crude oil continued to be the leading imports from SSA in 2016, predominantly from Nigeria, Angola, and Chad. The next leading imports were platinum, diamonds, vehicles and parts, and iron and steel from South Africa (valued at $6,759.20 million) and cocoa, rubber, and cashew nuts from Cote d'Ivoire (valued at $1,163.92 million). The value of the total US imports from SSA countries in the same year was $20.132 million, an increase of 7 percent from 2014. (See appendix E.)

The leading US exports to SSA countries in 2016 were concentrated in motor machinery, vehicles and parts, aircraft and parts, electrical machinery, and cereals. The top five SSA destinations for US exports were South Africa, Nigeria, Angola, Ghana, and Ethiopia. The value of the total US exports to SSA was $13,602 million, a decline of 24.48 percent from 2014. (See appendix E.)

Mattoo, Roy, and Subramanian provided a detailed analysis of the impact of AGOA on the apparel sector. Their study looked at both current trade and trade that would have resulted had all restrictions on SSA's exports being eliminated.[44] The restrictions focused on are the exclusion of some products from the scope of AGOA, and the imposition of stringent rules of origin requirements to qualify for the benefits under AGOA. With respect to current trade, the authors concluded that AGOA would raise the level of non-oil exports between 8 and 11 percent depending on the restrictiveness of the rules of origin in the non-apparel sector. Most of this increase is accounted for by the apparel sector, which is expected to see clothing exports raised by about 8.3 percent. In the case where there were no restrictions, non-oil exports would have been higher by about 43 percent. This means that AGOA, as it now stands, will yield only 19 to 26 percent of the benefits that could have been provided if access had been unconditional. Nearly 80 percent of the shortfall is accounted for by the rules of origin requirements in the apparel sector, which will significantly reduce exports below SSA's full potential.

Mattoo, Roy, and Subramanian noted that while the increases in exports are a small share of these countries' GDP, the trading opportunities provided by preferential access could be harnessed in a way that promotes long-run economic growth. They argued that AGOA has been a significant factor in the growth of the clothing industry in SSA, but the mandatory use of US fabrics (or limited regional fabric as inputs) raises SSA production costs, hence reducing the benefit of the preferences. Distance and relative efficiency considerations imply that China is likely the cheapest source of fabrics for SSA clothing producers. Clothing exports could have grown by close to 60 percent, had the rule of origin been removed.

While AGOA provides preferential access to US markets, the Act clearly comes with strings attached. The principal problem is with the rule of origin. The Economic Commission for Africa (ECA) has identified problems associated with the rule of origin as follows:

> To prevent third-world countries from passing their goods through AGOA beneficiary countries, a minimum amount of processing is necessary in the beneficiary country. However, the rules of origin for many products are difficult to meet. If production requires inputs that are not domestically available, they usually need to be imported from the preference-giving region, where they are more expensive than in third-world countries.[45]

As a result, the rule of origin reduces the benefit of the preferences and could lead to disincentives.

The rule of origin for apparel under AGOA is a departure from the rule of origin under the Cotonou Agreement, which governs preferential access to the EU. According to Mattoo, Davesh, and Aryind,

> The Cotonou rule of origin is based on the concept of "double transformation," that is, whereby if two of the processing stages (. . . weaving and assembly . . .) are done in the beneficiary country, duty-free entry into the EU can be enjoyed. Under Cotonou, therefore, yarn can be sourced from anywhere in the world, whereas under AGOA the yarn must come from a beneficiary SSA country or from the United States.[46]

Milan Vesely highlighted the economic payoff of AGOA with respect to textiles for the following countries: Madagascar, Kenya, Malawi, Mauritius and Swaziland. He noted that AGOA had achieved remarkable success in a short period of time since its establishment.[47] Under AGOA, Africa supplied 3.5 percent of all US textile imports, up from a low of 1.5 percent. As a result of AGOA, US imports from Africa have increased by 62 percent with textiles growing at a high rate of 25 percent. Furthermore, the Generalized System of Preference, which formed the basis of all AGOA regulations, has enabled US corporations to offer US consumers the benefits of lower prices and wider import choices.[48]

Ianchovichina, Mattoo, and Olarreaga assessed initiatives by the EU, Japan, and the United States to improve market access for the poorest countries. A sample of 37 SSA countries, many of which were AGOA beneficiaries, was analyzed. The study noted that improved market access for the poorest countries is widely seen as necessary to support their development efforts, as well as a critical element of a new development round or multilateral trade negotiations.[49] Preferential access benefits the SSA-37 recipients and improves their welfare because it leads to higher prices and quantities of their exports. On the other hand, the initiatives would hurt those developing countries that are excluded, because they get lower prices for their exports.[50]

The apparel sector is likely to expand, with the share of real value added generated in the sector increasing by a little over 3 percent. The reallocation of resources into apparel (and textiles) is likely to cause a small contraction in a range of these sectors. The welfare gains to SSA-37 are also small (0.02 percent) and the loss in tariff revenue for the United States is also negligible, 0.06 percent of total tariff revenue. Even if the United States were to grant duty-free access to all SSA-37 products—the most generous interpretation of the Trade and Development Act—the impact on export revenue and welfare of SSA-37 remains small. The gains are only about twice the gains arising from free access for apparel. In terms of sector value added, the expansion is still mostly in the apparel sector, with a small increase in the value added in the sugar-related sectors.[51] The results are not surprising given that these are really the only sectors where SSA-37 faces significant barriers in the US market.

The proposed liberalization of access to the EU market could, however, lead to much larger gains. An increase of around 2.8 percent of non-oil exports creates a 0.2 percent increase in welfare, six times larger than the gains from free access to the US market. The larger expansion is witnessed by the plant-based fibers, livestock, meat, and dairy products sectors, followed by the sugar-related sectors.[52]

The downside is that SSA-37 countries may be lured by current preferences to specialize in the production of products in which they do not have a global comparative advantage. As MFN tariffs decline over time and preference margins are eroded, these countries could suffer significant adjustment costs, and be even worse off because they have foregone opportunities to learn-by-doing in areas where they do have a comparative advantage.[53]

AGOA is also considered a unilateral position taken by the United States to further strip Africans of their democratic rights to determine an effective economic policy that will serve their interests.[54] The policy, it is argued, would lead to severe reduction in government spending and provide new rights for foreign investors to buy African natural resources and state firms. Furthermore, the policy would also impose US monopoly and patent rules upon Africa.[55] By calling for minimal government interference in the economy, through measures such as less price control, AGOA suggests the kind of interference that is objectionable. This could plausibly lead to an objection to SSA countries' regulation of FDI, such as regulating the transfer of licensing necessary for promoting the benefits of investment.[56] Similarly, Kaba offered cautionary comments on the rise of this partnership, noting that a US–African trade partnership has the potential of supplanting the Africa–EU trade partnership, which, he argued, has not benefited African countries over time. Nevertheless, he argued that the US–Africa trade partnership would only be realized if stakeholders such as African Americans continue to lobby for free trade between the United States and Africa.[57]

The major goal of AGOA is to promote trade and FDI in SSA countries. AGOA does offer some promise for trade expansion and investment in the region. In some of the countries, AGOA has increased exports to the United States in textiles and garments. FDI has also increased in the export sectors. For example, in the two years since its inception, AGOA helped stimulate FDI of $12.8 million in Kenya and $78 million in Mauritius, and helped create some 200,000 jobs in the apparel industry of the beneficiary countries.[58] The positive trade balance in beneficiary countries is an indication of increased FDI.

SUMMARY

Protectionist trade policies in industrial countries are among the factors that constrain exports and economic growth in developing countries. To assist African countries in their development efforts, US President William Clinton adopted the development paradigm that open trade helps to promote prosperity and peace worldwide. This paradigm supports Gibbon's claim that "concessions in the area of trade provide better long-term prospects for developing countries' economic development than do ones in aid."[59] Thus, on May 18, 2000, the president signed into law the AGOA that provides for duty-free treatment of certain products exported to the United States from approved beneficiary countries in SSA. The general intent of AGOA is to provide the beneficiary countries increased access to US markets and to promote FDI in exchange for making progress toward establishing a market economy, democratic institutions, and adherence to the rule of law among others.

AGOA has had mixed results. Overall, both the United States and beneficiary countries appear to have benefited from the Act. The combined values of the exports of AGOA countries to the United States have consistently exceed the combined values of their imports from the United States, indicating a positive trade balance in favor of the AGOA countries. At least in the case of trade in clothing, employment, and wage income gains can be expected in the developing countries.[60]

Despite the good intentions and benefits of AGOA, the policy has some challenges, such as the expiration of the Act itself, the rule of origin provisions, the need for diversification of trade in beneficiary countries, and reversion of democracy in some countries, such as Burundi and Sudan.[61] The frequent amendments and extensions of AGOA provisions may affect long-term investment in the region by creating uncertainty over the extent of future tariff preferences.

The rule of origin provisions seems to reduce the benefits of AGOA. According to the rule, if production requires inputs that are not domestically available, they usually need to be imported from the preference-giving country, where they are more expensive than in uninvolved countries. Combined with complex administrative requirements and red tape, including documentation of origin, the effect is to reduce investment in activities that could in principle benefit from preferences. As a result, this reduces the benefits of AGOA.

Diversification is also needed in the products and in the countries that benefit from AGOA. In 2016, the leading US imports under AGOA were energy-related products, transportation equipment, minerals, and textiles. These industries are very capital intensive and thus do not provide extensive employment opportunities for workers. Moreover, AGOA benefits are concentrated in a few countries with large proportion of the AGOA imports by the United States originating in Nigeria, South Africa, and Angola.

Some countries that are eligible for AGOA do not export under the program, because they lack the technical capacity to produce some of the products. Hence, according to Hoekman, Ng, and Olarreaga, increased "market access without the ability to produce profitability for export is of limited use," and market access should be complemented by efforts to improve the capacity of AGOA beneficiary countries to use trade as part of a sustained growth strategy.[62]

The burden of external debt can be a major impediment to economic growth and poverty reduction in many of the poorest countries in the world. As discussed above, the burden of debt in most SSA countries has contributed to economic decline in the region. Having recognized the constraint of foreign debt, the US Congress has been working toward making "comprehensive debt relief" available to SSA countries.[63] For instance, since the end of January 2009, the IMF has granted debt relief to about twenty SSA countries through the Multilateral Debt Relief Initiative, which is intended to help certain low-income countries advance toward the United Nations' Millennium Development Goals of halving poverty by 2015.[64] Such reliefs are designed to strengthen and expand the private sector, encourage increased trade and investment, support the development of free markets, and promote broad-scale economic growth in beneficiary countries."[65] The AGOA policy combined with other policies, such as debt relief, will further increase the levels of economic growth and development, as well as the welfare of the region.

NOTES

1. Constitutive Act of the African Union 2002. http://www.au2002.gov.za/docs/key_oau/au_act.htm. Retrieved August 1, 2006.
2. D. Moyo, *Dead Aid: Why Aid is Not Working and How There is a Better Way for Africa* (Vancouver, BCV: Douglas & McIntyre, 2009).
3. Moyo, *Dead Aid: Why Aid is Not Working and How There is a Better Way for Africa.*
4. Mbaku, "Entrenching Economic Freedom in Africa," 220–21.
5. Paul Collier and Jan Willem Gunning, "Explaining African Economic Performance," *Journal of Economic Literature* 37 (1999), 64–111.
6. Paul Bennell, "Foreign Direct Investment in Africa: Rhetoric and Reality," *SIAS Review* 17, no. 2 (1997), 127–29.
7. Sub-Saharan Africa is the region of the world that is most affected by HIV and AIDS. An estimated 22 million people are living with HIV at the end of 2007 and approximately 1.9 million new infections occurred during the year. http://www.Avert.org/aafrica. Retrieved October 22, 2008.
8. Ian Fergusson and Lenore M. Sek, "US Trade and Investment Relationship with Sub-Saharan Africa: The African Growth and Opportunity Act and Beyond," *Congressional Research Services*: *The Library of Congress* (March 10, 2003), 9–10.
9. Ibid.
10. Ibid.
11. Dara Carr, "Improving the Health of the World's Poorest People," *Health Bulletin* 1 (2004), 2.
12. Bennell, "Foreign Direct Investment in Africa: Rhetoric and Reality," 127–29.
13. Peter Gibbon, "African Growth and Opportunity Act and the Global Commodity Chain for Clothing," *World Development* 31, no. 11 (2003), 1809–27.
14. Rodney Slater, "Promoting Trade and Investment in Africa," *Economic Perspectives. US Information Agency Electronic Journal* 4, no. 3 (August 1999), 3–5.

15. Rebecca Trent, “Implications for Foreign Direct Investment in Sub-Saharan Africa under the African Growth and Opportunity Act,” *Northwestern Journal of International Law & Business* 123, no. 1 (Fall 2002), 213–37; AkJ. M. Migai Akech, “The African Growth and Opportunity Act: Implications for Kenya’s Trade and Development,” *New York Journal of International Law and Politics* 32 (2001): 651–53.

16. Whitney Schneidman, “President Clinton’s Partnership Initiative,” *Economic Perspective* 4, no. 3 (1999), 11–13.

17. Trent, “Implications for Foreign Direct Investment in Sub-Saharan Africa,” 213–37.

18. Charles A. Whittier, “The African Growth and Opportunity Act: A Cup Half Empty or Half Full?” *Black Business Journal* (1998), 1–5. http://www.bjoline.com/archives/Africa Growth.html. Retrieved May 29, 2004.

19. International Trade Administration, “Summary of AGOA I.” http://trade.gov/agoa/legislation/index.asp. Retrieved September 9, 2016.

20. See Office of the United States Trade Representative. http://www.ustr.gov/Trade_Development/Preference_Programs/Section_Index.html. Retrieved October 25, 2008.

21. Aaditya Mattoo, Davesh Roy, and Arvind Subramanian, “The Africa Growth and Opportunity Act and Its Rules of Origin: Generosity Undermined?” *World Economy* 26, no. 6 (2003): 829–51.

22. Ibid.

23. Ibid., 831.

24. Ibid., 836.

25. Gibbon, “African Growth and Opportunity Act and the Global Commodity Chain for Clothing,” 1809–27.

26. 108th Congress of the United States. “H.R. 4103 AGOA Acceleration Act of 2004” (January 20, 2004), 7–8.

27. Gibbon, “African Growth and Opportunity Act and the Global Commodity Chain for Clothing,” 1810.

28. “The Act authorizes the President to designate countries as eligible to receive the benefits of AGOA if they are determined to have established, or are making continual progress toward establishing the following: market-based economies; the rule of law and political pluralism; elimination of barriers to US trade and investment; protection of intellectual property; efforts to combat corruption; policies to reduce poverty, increasing availability of health care and educational opportunities; protection of human rights and worker rights; and elimination of certain child labor practices.” “These criteria have been embraced overwhelmingly by the vast majority of African nations, which are striving to achieve the objectives although none is expected to have fully implemented the entire list.” http://www.agoa.gov/eligibility/country_eligibility.html. Retrieved May 28, 2007.

29. James Fisher-Thompson, “Africa: A Top Policy Priority in the New Bush Strategy Plan,” *US Foreign Policy Agenda* 7, no. 4 (2002).

30. Gibbon, “African Growth and Opportunity Act and the Global Commodity Chain for Clothing,” 1810–11.

31. On January 18, 2001, Swaziland was designated as the thirty-fifth AGOA eligible country and on May 16, 2002 Côte d’Ivoire was designated as the thirty-sixth

eligible country. On January 1, 2003 The Gambia and the Democratic Republic of Congo were designated as the thirty-seventh and thirty-eighth. On January 1, 2004, Angola was designated as AGOA eligible; however, effective January 1, 2004, the President removed the Central African Republic and Eritrea from the list of eligible countries. On December 10, 2004, the President designated Burkina Faso as AGOA eligible. Effective January 1, 2005, the President removed Côte d'Ivoire from the list of eligible countries. Effective January 1, 2006, the President designated Burundi as AGOA eligible and removed Mauritania from the list. Effective December 29, 2006, the President designated Liberia as AGOA eligible.

32. http://www.agoa.gov/eligibility/country_eligibility.html.

33. The White House Press Release, "To Take Certain Actions under the African Growth and Opportunity Act," President G. W. Bush Remarks at the signing of the AGOA Acceleration Act of 2004. http://www.whitehouse.gov/news/releases/2004/12/20041221-9.html. Akech, "The African Growth and Opportunity Act," 700.

34. Melina Platas (Friday, November 21, 2008) "President Obama." http://www.independent.co.ug/index.php/reports/special-report/71-special-report/283-president-obama?tmpl=component&print=1&page=. Retrieved March 18, 2009.

35. Honorable Uhuru Kenyatta, Kenya, Office of the Deputy Prime Minister and Ministry of Trade, "Speech by the Incoming of the AGOA African Consultative Group," July 14, 2008. http://democracy-africa.org/agoacsonet/KenyaDPM2008AGOAStatement.pdf. Retrieved March 18, 2009.

36. Rosa Whitaker, the Whitaker Group, a consulting group specializing in trade with Africa. http://www.politifact.com/truth-o-meter/promises/obameter/promise/429/strengthen-the-african-growth-and-opportunity-act/.

37. http://www.politifact.com/truth-o-meter/promises/obameter/promise/429/strengthen-the-african-growth-and-opportunity-act/.

38. Ibid.

39. "US-Africa Trade Gets a Boost With Renewal of AGOA," *The Wall Street Journal*, June 25, 2015. http://blogs.wsj.com/frontiers/2015/06/25/us-africa-trade-gets-a-boost-with-renewal-of-agoa/. Retrieved September 13, 2015.

40. Office of the United States Trade Representative. Opening Statement of USTR Robert Lighthizer at 2017 AGOA Forum. https://ustr.gov/about-us/policy-offices/press-office/press-releases/2017/august/opening-statement-ustr-robert. Retrieved January 22, 2018.

41. Akech, "The African Growth and Opportunity Act," 651–53.

42. Ibid.

43. "United States Department of Commerce, International Trade Administration," *U.S.-Trade Profile*. Washington, DC, 2007. http://www.agoa.gov/resources/US-African%20Trade%20Profile%202008%20-%20Final.pdf. Retrieved March 14, 2009.

44. Mattoo, Roy, and Subramanian, "The Africa Growth and Opportunity Act and Its Rules of Origin: Generosity Undermined?" 829–51.

45. UNECA, "*Meeting the Challenges of Unemployment and Poverty in Africa,*" 43.

46. Mattoo et al. "The Africa Growth and Opportunity Act and Its Rules of Origin," 837.

47. Milan Vesely, "AGOA: The Nuts and Bolts," *African Business* (2003), 30–32.
48. Ibid.
49. Elena Ianchovichina, Aaditya Mattoo and Marcelo Olarrega, "Unrestricted Market Access for Sub-Saharan Africa: How Much Is It Worth and Who Pays?" World Bank Development Research Working Paper No. 2595, 1–30.
50. Ibid., 7–8.
51. Ibid., 16.
52. Ibid., 2.
53. Ibid., 22.
54. William Martin, "Dictated Trade: The Case Against the African Growth and Opportunity Act," *Review of African Political Economy* 27, no. 77 (1998), 531–32.
55. Ibid.
56. Akech, "The African Growth and Opportunity Act," 700.
57. Amadu Jacky Kaba, "Africa-US Partnership in the 21st Century," *Chimera: US African Institute* 2, no. 1 (2004), 18–25.
58. United Nations Conference on Trade and Development, "World Investment Report, 2003, FDI Policies for Development: National and International Perspective," United Nations, New York, and Geneva (2003), 37.
59. Gibbon, "African Growth and Opportunity Act and the Global Commodity Chain for Clothing," 1824.
60. Ibid.
61. The discussion of these challenges is drawn extensively from Fergusson and Sek, Report for Congress, Congressional Research Service, The Library of Congress, Order Code RL 31772, March 10, 2003.
62. Hoekman, Bernard, Francis Ng, and Marcelo Olarreaga, "Eliminating Excessive Tariffs on Exports of Least Developed Countries," *The World Bank Economic Reviews* 16, no. 1 (2002), 19.
63. The African Growth and Opportunity Act, Section 121 (1) (a), (1) (b) (1). http://www.ustr.gov/assets/Document_Library/Reports_Publications/2005/asset_upload_file604_7857.pdf.
64. International Monetary Fund (IMF), "The Multilateral Debt Initiative." http://www.imf.org/external/np/exr/facts/mdri.htm. Retrieved March 17, 2009. The IMF has granted debt relief to the following SSA countries: Benin Burkina Faso, Burundi, Cameroon, The Gambia, Ghana, Madagascar, Malawi, Mali, Mauritania, Mozambique, Niger, Rwanda, Sao Tome and Principe, Senegal, Sierra Leone, Tanzania, Uganda, and Zambia.
65. Fergusson and Sek, "US Trade and Investment Relationship with Sub-Saharan Africa."

Chapter 7

Democracy and Governance in Africa

The Continental Perspective

Since the late 1950s, African countries have struggled for independence and have also faced the challenge of promoting democracy and good governance. As many of the countries gained independence, their leaders realized that through a unified body or organization of their countries they could hasten the independence of other countries on the continent. To this effect, the representatives of independent African countries, numbering more than thirty at that time, gathered in Addis Ababa, Ethiopia, and established the Organization of African Unity (OAU) in 1963. According to the charter of the organization, achieving freedom, equality, justice, and dignity are the legitimate aspirations of the African peoples. The aims and objectives of the organization were, among others, to:

1. Promote the unity and solidarity of African states;
2. Co-ordinate and intensify their cooperation and efforts to achieve a better life for the peoples of Africa;
3. Defend their sovereignty, territorial integrity, and independence and eradicate all forms of colonialism from Africa;
4. Promote international cooperation, giving due regard to the Charter of the United Nations and the Universal Declaration of Human Rights; and
5. Co-ordinate and harmonize members' political, diplomatic, economic, educational, cultural, health, welfare, scientific, technical, and defense policies.[1]

The organization has been adopting various initiatives to achieve its aim and objectives. However, ideological differences among member states have often made agreement on a single course of action difficult. For example, the absence of an armed force similar to the United Nations' peacekeeping contingents left the organization with no means to enforce its edicts. The unwillingness to intervene in the internal affairs of member nations often meant the OAU would not confront brutal dictatorships, such as the Idi Amin regime in Uganda, or domestic crises, such as the Rwandan Genocide, thereby prompting some observers to criticize the organization as a forum for rhetoric rather than action.

Recognizing this and other shortcomings, the OAU issued the Sirte Declaration in Sirte, Libya in September 1999, calling for a new body to take its place. In July 2000 at Lomé Togo, the Constitutive Act of the African Union established the African Union and set out the codified framework under which the African Union is to function. On July 9, 2002, the African Union was launched in South Africa as a continental body. The various initiatives and substantial progress in many areas paved the way for the establishment of the AU, which continues to this day uphold many of the founding principles of the OAU. One of its key objectives is to promote democratic principles and institutions, popular participation, and good governance. To achieve these objectives the AU has undertaken the implementation of initiatives that were established before and after its establishment. Noteworthy among those initiatives that focus on democratic principles, popular participation, and good governance are the following:

1. The African Charter on Human and People's Rights (1981);
2. OAU Declaration on the Political and Socio-Economic Situation in Africa and the Fundamental Changes taking place in the World (1990): which underscored Africa's resolve to seize the initiative to determine its destiny and to address the challenges to peace, democracy and security;
3. The Charter on Popular Participation adopted in 1990: a testimony to the renewed determination of the OAU to endeavor to place the African citizen at the center of development and decision making;
4. The Mechanism for Conflict Prevention, Management and Resolution (1993): a practical expression of the determination of the African leadership to find solutions to conflicts, promote peace, security, and stability in Africa;
5. The Algiers Decision on Unconstitutional Changes of Government (1999) and the Lomé Declaration on the framework for an OAU Response to Unconstitutional Changes (2000);
6. The 2000 Solemn Declaration on the Conference on Security, Stability, Development and Cooperation: establishes the fundamental principles for the promotion of Democracy and Good Governance in the Continent;
7. Sirte Declaration was issued in Libya in 1999 calling for the establishment of an African Union, with a view, to accelerating the process of integrating the continent to play its rightful role in the global economy;

8. The NEPAD: adopted as a Program of the AU at the Lusaka Summit (2001); and
9. African Charter on Democracy, Elections, and Governance on January 30, 2007.

THE MONROVIA COLLOQUIUM AND THE LAGOS PLAN OF ACTION

The foundation of the initiatives for the achieving the aims and objectives of the OAU included the Monrovia Colloquium and the Lagos Plan of Action. The OAU and the United Nations Economic Commission for Africa conveyed a meeting in February 1979 in Monrovia, Liberia, where they outlined the development strategies for Africa. This meeting, which was referred to as the Monrovia Colloquium, outlined the following strategies for development:

1. Give an important role to the field of human resources development by promoting the elimination of illiteracy;
2. Put science and technology in the service of development by reinforcing the autonomous capacity of our countries in this filed;
3. Achieve self-sufficiency in food production and supply;
4. Implement completely the programs for the United Nations Transport and Communications Decade for Africa;
5. Realize the sub-regional and regional internally-located industrial development;
6. Cooperate in the field of national resources control exploration extraction and use for the development of our economies for the benefit of our peoples and to set up appropriate institutions to achieve these purposes;
7. Develop indigenous entrepreneurship technical manpower, technological abilities to enable our peoples to assume greater responsibility for the achievement of our individual and collective development goals;
8. Cooperate in the prevention, protection, and improvement of the natural environment; and
9. Ensure that our development policies reflect adequately our socio-cultural values to reinforce our cultural identity.[2]

In addition to the strategies laid out in the Monrovia Colloquium, the OAU adopted the Lagos Plan of Action in 1980 at an extraordinary session of the African Heads and Governments. The plan included a framework for African development and the title became the Lagos Plan of Action for the Economic Development of Africa (1980–2000).[3] The Lagos Plan provided a list of the factors that African leaders considered as impediment to Africa's development:

1. The lack of self-reliance;
2. Partial disengagement from the world economy and expansion of intra-African trade;
3. Economic cooperation on a regional and sub-regional basis;
4. Self-sufficiency in foodstuffs especially in cereals, in livestock and in fish products; and
5. Balanced development involving all aspects of the African economies.[4]

However, the strategic development goals outlined in the Monrovia Colloquium and the Lagos Plan of Action have been difficult to attain. According to Adedeji, Terbia, and Bugembe (1991), the goals proved elusive because the colonial economic frame work inherited by most African states after independence was difficult to change radically to what the African government had called for in the LPA. After independence, most African leaders were familiar mainly with the colonial economic framework which focuses on public sector employment and bureaucratic public administration. In addition resources for national development plans and annual budgets of most African countries tended to encourage the dependency of their economies on developed countries.[5] The implementation of the LPA was also impeded by exogenous factors, such as structural and political obstacles—for instance, outward economic orientation and the lack of economic complementarity because of narrow economic base among the African countries. Their economies have been based on the exports of primary products, which are subject to global economic fluctuations. Extraneous factors such as drought had also impeded the implementation of some the agricultural goals.[6]

AFRICAN CHARTER ON HUMAN AND PEOPLES' RIGHTS

Although the strategic framework for development was presented in the Monrovia Plan and the LPA, some African states remained preoccupied with the struggle for independence during the Cold War period of the 1980s as states such as South Africa, and other frontline states such as Zimbabwe and Namibia were yet to attain independence, while other African states were preoccupied with Cold War alignment. Hence, the struggle for independence went beyond the watershed period of the 1960s. Given these challenges, the Assembly of Heads of State of the OAU at its sixteenth session held in Monrovia, Liberia from July 17 to 20, 1979, made the provision to prepare a preliminary draft on an African Charter on Human and Peoples' Rights providing inter alia for the establishment of bodies to promote and protect human and peoples' rights. Accordingly the African Charter on Human and People's Rights was adopted on June 27, 1981, and entered into force on October 21, 1986. The African leaders pledged to protect and promote human rights and reaffirmed the OAU commitment to the eradication of all forms of colonialism while at the same time agitating for better lives for the peoples of the continent.[7] According to Article 2 of the charter:

> Every individual shall be entitled to the enjoyment of the rights and freedoms recognized and guaranteed in the present Charter without distinction of any kind such as race, ethnic group, color, sex, language, religion, political or any other opinion, national and social origin, fortune, birth or other status.[8]

Moreover, at the end of the Cold War, the issue of democratic consolidation, good governance, and human rights have become the preoccupation of most African states.

African leaders have concluded that good governance and economic development cannot take place in an environment of conflicts. They recognized the need to promote conflict resolution between nations, ethnic, and regional groupings. Accordingly, these leaders adopted the 1993 Declaration on establishing the Mechanism for Conflict Prevention, Management, and Resolution. At the sub-regional level, the ECOWAS also established a mechanism for collective security and peace known as "Mechanism for Conflict Prevention, Management, Resolution, Peace-keeping and Security" in Togo in 1999. In 2000 the African leaders also adopted the Solemn Declaration on the Conference on Security, Stability, Development and Cooperation to promote democratic principles and institutions, popular participation and good governance in the continent. Through the Solemn Declaration of Government, African leaders further acknowledged that the security, stability, and development of every African country is inseparably linked to that of other African countries. Instability in one country affects the stability in neighboring countries and has serious implications for continental unity, peace, and development. For instance, the civil war that began in Liberia in the late 1980s had a spillover effect in neighboring countries, such as Sierra Leone. According to the declaration, the peaceful resolution of disputes should be pursued with emphasis on seeking African solutions to African problems. The prevention, management, and resolution of conflicts provide the enabling environment for peace, security, stability, and development to flourish. They further acknowledge that democracy, good governance, respect for human and peoples' rights, and the rule of law are prerequisites for the security, stability, and development of the continent.

African governments undertook additional initiatives in promoting democratic development and the participation of people. These governments have been concerned about the serious deterioration in human and economic conditions in Africa in the decade of the 1980s, the lack of progress in achieving popular participation and the lack of full appreciation of the role of popular participation plays in the process of recovery and development. In response to this concern, in February 1990, the International Conference on Population Participation in the Recovery and Development Process in Africa was held in Tanzania in the search for a collective understanding of the role of popular participation in the development and transformation of the African region. The conference was also an occasion to give "renewed focus to the concepts of democratic development, people's solidarity and creativity, and self-reliance and to formulate policy recommendations for national governments, popular organizations, and the international community in order to strengthen participatory processes and patterns of development."[9] To this end, the conference adopted the African Charter for Popular Participation in Development and Transformation to foster popular participation and democratic development in wide range of entities that include the following:[10]

1. People and their organizations;
2. International community;
3. African and non-African NGOs and voluntary development organizations;
4. Media and communication;
5. Women's organizations;
6. Organized labor; and
7. Youth and students and their organizations.

African governments, though eager to attract financial assistance, face tangible pressures to move toward more open and competitive political regimes. Moreover, since the end of the Cold War, democracies are more likely to be rewarded with resources and legitimacy, while governments in nondemocratic regimes find the global environment more uncomfortable. For instance, US President Barack visited Ghana to legitimize Ghana's democratic governance in Africa. As a result, African leaders pledged to work, both individually and collectively, to promote these principles in their countries, sub-regions, and the continent.[11] The pledge is made in a document known as the NEPAD.

THE NEW PARTNERSHIP FOR AFRICA'S DEVELOPMENT

NEPAD, which emanated from the OAU, was adopted by the Assembly of African Heads of State and Government in 2001 African leaders undertook to promote and protect democracy and human rights in their respective countries and regions, by developing clear standards of accountability and participatory governance at the national and sub-regional levels. NEPAD also adopted the MDGs as a core component of its goals.[12] NEPAD's development goals for Africa differ only marginally from the MDGs report.[13] NEPAD seeks to deal with the continent's underdevelopment as a collective effort by addressing its poor economic performance.[14] The idea of developing a new agenda for African recovery dates back to 1999 when the Millennium Partnership for the African Recovery Programmed (MAP) was borne out of the OAU Summit held in Libya in September 1999.[15] Since then various African leaders developed a number of plans, which were finally consolidated into the new initiative called NEPAD in October 2001 at the Lusaka Conference of the OAU. There, African heads of states signed the NEPAD as a blueprint for addressing Africa's development challenges. NEPAD calls for a reversal of this process through a new partnership between Africa and the international community.[16] The objective of NEPAD is poverty reduction, which is made clear in the opening line of the NEPAD document as follows:

> This new African initiative is a pledge by African leaders, based on a common vision and a firm and shared conviction, that they have a pressing duty to eradicate poverty and to place their countries, both individually and collectively, on a path of sustainable growth and development, and at the same time to participate actively in the world economy and body politic.[17]

To achieve the objectives of poverty reduction, African leaders have identified certain programs for which they will jointly take responsibility. A key component of these programs is "promoting and protecting democracy and human rights in their respective countries and regions by developing clear standards of accountability, transparency, and participatory governance at the national and sub-national levels."[18] African leaders have realized that democracy and good governance are essential conditions for sustainable development (NEPAD, 2001). NEPAD, with its emphasis on democracy and good governance, reflects an emerging inclination among some African governments to embrace these tendencies. As one writer put it, "democracy is an avenue by which their legitimate aspiration for a better future can be expressed and claims for redress made."[19]

The rest of the programs identified in NEPAD are as follows:

1. Strengthening the mechanisms for conflict prevention, management, and resolution in the region;
2. Restoring and maintaining macroeconomic stability;
3. Instituting transparent legal and regulatory frameworks for financial markets and audition of private firms and the public sector;

4. Revitalizing and extending the provision of education and health services;
5. Promoting the role of women in socioeconomic development;
6. Building state capacity to enforce the legal framework and maintain law and order; and
7. Promote the development of infrastructure.[20]

Although the document does not state the priorities of the issues that should be addressed, the initiating presidents proposed that the following programs be fast-tracked, in collaboration with development partners:

1. Communicable diseases—HIV/AIDS, malaria, and tuberculosis;
2. Information and communications technology;
3. Debt reduction; and
4. Market access.[21]

The NEPAD document was developed within the context of the United Nations Millennium Declaration adopted in September 2000. NEPAD is based on the theory that the underdevelopment and marginalization of the continent could be addressed by improvements in trade, aid, and capital flows. In NEPAD, quantitative goals are set, such as achieving an average annual economic growth rate of 7 percent per annum and reducing poverty by 2015.[22] To achieve this, it believes that Africa needs to fill an annual resource gap of 12 percent of GDP, or US$64 billion. NEPAD was an arrangement through which African leaders would promote good governance and human rights in return for increase in trade and investment in the amount of US$64 billion per year from the West.[23] Although it is recognized that part of this resource gap could be filled by increases in domestic savings and improvements in public revenue collection, the bulk of the resources would have to be obtained from external sources, particularly debt relief, as well as in aid, trade, and FDI flows.[24]

The NEPAD framework for resources for Africa's development envisaged that the mobilization of resources would be undertaken through two mainstream initiatives: the capital flow initiative and market institution initiative.[25] The capital flows initiative emphasizes the importance of increases in domestic mobilization, debt relief, official development assistance, and FDI flows as measures to enhance mobilization of resources. The market access initiative emphasizes the importance of the diversification of production, the promotion of the role of private sector, the removal of non-tariff barriers, and the promotion of African exports through intra-African trade to the rest of the world. These two initiatives are essential for economic growth and development.

AN ASSESSMENT OF NEPAD

A review of the implementation of NEPAD has produced mixed results. NEPAD has its staunch supporters and its critics. Professor Ravi Kanpur has suggested three keys questions that should be addressed in determining the priorities and evaluation of programs in NEPAD as follows:

1. Is the program particularly well suited to a regional organization, and are there no other regional organizations that are already doing it reasonably well?
2. Is the program particularly well suited to a regional organization that is rooted in democratic values?
3. Does the program combine both direct and indirect benefits to the poor?

Programs and actions which score high should be prioritized on the NEPAD agenda. Those that score low should instead be implemented by other regional organizations to avoid duplication of efforts. For example, according to Kanpur, the Peace and Security Initiative score very highly on all three criteria. Actions for this initiative are expected in four areas: (1) prevention, management, and resolution of conflict; (2) peacemaking and peace enforcement; (3) post-conflict reconciliation, rehabilitation, and reconstruction; and (4) combating illicit proliferation of small arms, light weapons, and landmines. The proposed actions are regional in scope and therefore require a regional organization formed and supported by democratic governments. The same applies to the actions proposed under the Democracy and Political Governance Initiative, which are: (1) a series of commitments by participating countries to create or consolidate basic governance processes and practices; (2) an undertaking by participating countries to take the lead in supporting initiatives that foster governance; and (3) the institutionalization of commitments through the NEPAD leadership to ensure that the core values of the initiative are abided by.

On the other hand, actions required under the Economic and Comparative Governance Initiative may not be suited to NEPAD's comparative advantage. The actions are: (1) a task force from Ministries of Finance and Central Banks to provide advice on appropriate standards and good practice; (2) recommendations by the Implementation Committee to states for implementation; (3) countries will develop a program for improving public financial management and targets; and (4) heads of State Implementation Committee to mobilize resources for capacity-building to enable countries to comply with mutually agreed minimum standards and codes of conduct. While these proposed actions are important and have some regional dimensions, they may be better suited for implementation by other organizations such as the African Development Bank. Moreover, it is not clear how country-specific agreements with international financial institutions will interact with the region-wide initiatives in economic management.

The launch of the African Union in South Africa in July 2002, whereby it replaced the OAU, presents an interesting juncture in recent African history. Certainly, as the AU redefines the nature of the relationship between African countries, with a vision for continental integration, an opportunity presents itself for the continent to shed its past and adopt a new development path. There is a clear intention that NEPAD should be the development plan for the AU, but begs various questions because the relationship between this plan and this body is unclear.[26]

NEPAD has been criticized by some as having a neoliberal slant. NEPAD declares Africa open for business, and this is a deep-seated paradigm shift from the inward-looking statism of the past. The document emphasizes the importance of markets and of providing an environment conducive to FDI. It asks the global community to enter a partnership with the continent on an equal footing because it is in their interests to do so, it envisages the following responsibilities for the developed world:

1. Support materially the mechanisms for conflict resolution in Africa;
2. Accelerate debt reduction for highly indebted African countries and reverse the declines in official development assistance (ODA);
3. Improve African terms of trade and market access;
4. Encourage investment in Africa;
5. Secure access to essential drugs for Africans suffering from infectious disease;
6. Promote technological advancement on the continent; and
7. Ensure that the World Bank and other multilateral development finance institutions participate as investors in key economic infrastructure projects.[27]

A number of concerns about how the annual resource gap of 12 percent, or $65 billion, will be raised. For example:

1. It offers very little by way of assisting Africa to become more self-reliant in financing;
2. It does not provide any ideas regarding improving Africa's weak financial institutions, particularly the African Development Bank;
3. It does not outline any business plan for its priority projects; and
4. It does not say anything about a contingency plan if donor countries are not forthcoming with the required resources.[28]

When NEPAD was launched in 2001, it was championed as Africa's own development plan. While the initiative is widely regarded as a welcomed sign of the continent's renewed commitment to peace, democracy, and good governance, the financial resources required to implement the program have raised doubt about the extent to which NEPAD can be a partnership of equality. An additional capital flow of $64 billion a year is required for the program's success, and while NEPAD maintains that Africa is not appealing 'for further entrenchment of dependency through aid', the bulk of the resources would have to come from development assistance, especially given the continent's low level of FDI.[29] Thus, critics regard this dependency on foreign assistance as an indication that NEPAD is not actually owned by Africans at all. As one critic noted,

> NEPAD represents at best a few elite Africans who have internalized Western values and dressed them in an African garb; a 'western wolf in African sheepskin.' At worst, it is 'neo-liberal project through which the Western world would like to not only promote their strategic and national security interests, but also ensure perpetuation of Africa's dependent development under globalization.'[30]

In fact, some Western countries are not meeting their financial commitments made to African countries. At the G8 summit held in Canada in June 2002, the industrialized countries committed themselves to only a fraction of the resources that NEPAD is requesting.[31] Additionally, at the 2005 Gleneagles summit in Scotland, the G8 countries pledged to increase aid to Africa by $22 billion to $25 billion by 2010 to fight poverty—more than doubling the 2004 level of aid to the continent. Out of this amount pledged, only about a third ($7 billion) has been paid. A report on how much aid the world's eight leading economies give to Africa states that Italy and France are failing to keep their promises. The report, backed by Bill Gates of Microsoft Corporation and Archbishop Desmond Tutu, states that Italy has cut back on how much it gives, despite ambitious pledges made at the G8 summit in 2005. The cut in payment may be partly attributed to the global financial crises. Former United Nations secretary general Kofi Annan, along with musician turned anti-poverty campaigner, Bob Geldof, noted that "the world's poorest people have benefited least from globalization, but they are now suffering the most from a crisis they did not cause."[32]

Moreover, Africa's dependence on development assistance is contrary to the objectives of AGOA to which it subscribed. As discussed above, to assist SSA countries in their development, United States President William Jefferson Clinton adopted a development paradigm that opened trade to promote prosperity and peace rather than promoting aid. Thus, in 2000, the president signed into law the AGOA. The overall goal of AGOA was to provide SSA beneficiary countries increased access to the US market and to promote FDI in exchange for making progress toward establishing a market economy, democratic institutions, and adherence to the rule of law, among others. It now appears that NEPAD is a reversion to the development strategy that relied on global capital and dependent development that AGOA was designed to prevent. Moreover, most of the African countries whose debt was forgiven began borrowing at very high rates.

One of the harshest criticisms launched against NEPAD is based on the way in which African leaders responded, or failed to respond, to the questionable Zimbabwe elections in 2002. In this election, the incumbent president of twenty-two years, Robert Mugabe, unleashed his supporters and paramilitary force on the supporters of the opposition candidate, killing and wounding many of them. Yet, many African leaders failed to take any actions against Mugabe for such atrocities. This highlights the weakness of NEPAD. This threatened to undermine Africa's attempt to promote democracy and good governance. Decades later, the military removed Mugabe from power through a coup in November 2017, after serving as president for thirty-seven years. As one writer put it, "One renegade country did enormous damage to the entire continent and put the [NEPAD] plan in question in the G8." The industrialized countries responded by querying the very basis of NEPAD and Africa's commitment to it. These criticisms against NEPAD can be summarized as follows:

> That it is now effectively dead can be in no doubt. Numerous conversations with diplomats from the main Western countries confirm this, with NEPAD being variously described as an "irrelevancy," a "pipe dream," and as having been "killed by Mugabe." Indeed, the Zimbabwe factor and the outright refusal by the NEPAD's key promoters to adhere to their own rhetoric regarding democracy and good governance has made NEPAD little more than the butt of jokes in many quarters. News that in February 2003 Mbeki and Obasanjo were trying to block Zimbabwe's continued suspension from the Commonwealth and support Mugabe's readmission was not only not particularly surprising, given their antics over the last eighteen months, but also fitted a well-worn pattern that has staked out the history of NEPAD since its launch.[33]

Moreover, the AU includes states whose governance and practices are inconsistent with the objectives and principles of the AU. Maloka (2002) notes that the dilemma is whether such member states should be excluded from the Union along the lines of NEPAD or whether they should be provided with a window period allowing them to institute the necessary reforms that will align their countries with the provisions of the AU Constitutive Act. This view, however, may threaten the existence of NEPAD. In an effort to strengthen the NEPAD agreement of 2001, NEPAD Planning and Coordinating Agency developed a strategic plan to cover the period of 2014 through 2017. The plan envisioned would be driven by the core principles of leadership, ownership and participation.[34]

Despite the slow contribution of NEPAD to democratization, African leaders continued their commitment to democracy. At the 36th Ordinary Session meeting of the AU, the participants reiterated the importance of the previous instruments and initiatives that the OAU adopted with the aim of deepening and consolidating democracy, as well as adherence to human rights on the continent. They emphasized that strict observance of these instruments would significantly reduce the risk of unconstitutional changes of governments and popular uprisings on the continent.[35] Some of the instruments mentioned included the 2000 Solemn Declaration of the Conference on Security, Stability, Cooperation and Development, African Charter on Human and Peoples' Rights, the African Charter on Democracy, Elections and Governance, and the OAU Declaration on the Principles Governing Democratic Elections in Africa.

African leaders have also realized that a major threat to democratic consolidation on the continent is the forcible removal of heads of states and government. In response, the OAU adopted the Declaration on the Unconstitutional Changes in Government in Lomé, Togo, in 2000. The unconstitutional changes of government and popular uprisings were considered to be deeply rooted in governance deficiencies, such as greed, corruption, selfishness, marginalization, abuse of human rights, refusal to accept electoral defeat, and manipulation of constitution, as well as unconstitutional review of constitutions to serve narrow interest. AU member states were to deepen the culture of democracy, accountability, inclusiveness, participation, reconciliation, and good governance to foster peace and stability on the continent.[36]

On January 30, 2007, the African Union adopted the framework for consolidation of democracy, elections, and governance in Africa through the Charter on Democracy, Elections, and Governance. The AU Charter was entered into force on February 15, 2012, and the last signature was on April 21, 2017.[37] Articles three and four of the charter provide additional emphasis on democracy through free and fair elections and popular participation. The principle of Article three focused on the principle of regular and fair elections:

1. Respect for human rights and democratic principles;
2. Access to and exercise of state power in accordance with the constitution of the state party and the principle of the rule of law;
3. Promotion of a system of government that is representative; and
4. Holding of regular, transparent, free, and fair elections.[38]

The principle of Article four emphasized the rule of law and human rights. The basic tenants of this article are the following:

1. State parties shall commit themselves to promote democracy, the principle of the rule of law and human rights; and
2. State parties shall recognize popular participation through universal suffrage as the alienable right of the people.[39]

Sporadic occurrences of unconstitutional change of government continue to set back democracy on the continent. For example in November 2017, the Zimbabwean military forcibly removed their ninety-seven-year-old president who had served for thirty-seven years. Elections in Kenya were also marred by uprising and irregularities in 2017. The presidential election held in Liberia in October 2017 took many weeks to produce the final results after several legal challenges.

SUMMARY

After more than a half century since independence, an assessment of democratic governance in Africa is important, overall trends in democratic governance in Africa has been positive although with sporadic occurrences of nondemocratic practices in some countries.[40] On average, significant progress has been made in promoting democratic governance. According to Engle Bert, "there is no doubt that . . . on the average, African countries are more democratic now than they were before 1990 . . . from being on the average as not free in the 1970s Africans are now partly free."[41] The number of African states in which the governments have been defeated at the ballot box has increased significantly since the 1990s. For example, recent transfers of power have been democratic in Gambia, Ghana, Nigeria, and Liberia. Today, almost every state except Eritrea has held elections of some form. However, while this represents a remarkable turn of events, the average quality of these elections and the level of civil liberties appear to be declining on the continent. According to the National Elections across Democracy and Autocracy dataset, on a 1 to 10 scale, in which 10 is the best score possible, African elections average just over 5.

In many countries, leaders who were never committed to respecting a two-term (or in some cases three-term) limit have been able to change or reinterpret the law in a way that allows them to remain in office indefinitely. As a result, term limits have been overturned in Burundi, Cameroon, Chad, Republic of Congo (also known as Congo-Brazzaville), Djibouti, Gabon, Guinea, Namibia, Rwanda, Sudan, Togo, and Uganda. Authoritarian regimes continue to monopolize power in countries like Burundi and Zambia thereby resisting the promotion of democracy. In Cameroon, President Biya has ruled for more than thirty years. Some of these regimes are a result of sporadic military coups as in Egypt and Zimbabwe. In the case of Zimbabwe, in 2017 the military overthrew the ninety-seven-year-old President Robert Mugabe, who had ruled the country for thirty-seven years. He had refused to hold free and fair elections making it difficult for oppositions to win elections.

However, one of the most important democratic institutions of them all is starting to take root in a number of states. For example, presidents have accepted—or been forced to accept—the ultimate check on their authority in Benin, Botswana, Burkina Faso, Cape Verde, Ghana, Kenya, Mali, Malawi, Mozambique, Nigeria, São Tomé and Príncipe, Sierra Leone, Tanzania, and Zambia.

After many decades of various attempts and the commitment of vast resources of several international organizations and governments, Africa still faces challenges in promoting democratic governance. African leaders have come to the realization that good governance and democracy are necessary for sustainable development of African states. Democracy provides an institutional platform for improved economic performance.[42] African leaders have therefore pledged to achieve this through the formulation and implementation of various initiatives. These initiatives have included various charters such as African Charter for Popular Participation in Development and Transformation, the African Charter on Democracy, Elections and Governance, and NEPAD. Through NEPAD, African leaders have embarked on a broader and participatory approach to Africa's commitment in promoting good governance and democracy. As President Barack Obama of the United States stated cogently during his visit to Ghana on July 11, 2009, "Africa's future is up to Africans."[43] And Professor Lloyd Dumas further notes, "It is long past time for Africans to take control of their future . . . by moving in directions that will create a political and economic environment in which the inherent creativity and intellectual capability of the African people can flourish." Democracy and development are key to the creation of such an environment. Political will and good governance are indispensable to realizing democratic governance in Africa.

NOTES

1. The Organization of African Unity. http://www.dirco.gov.za/foreign/Multilateral/africa/oau.htm.

2. Adedeji, Teriba, and Bugembe, *The Challenge of African Economic Recovery and Development*, 132.

3. Robert S. Browne and Robert J. Cummings, *The Lagos Plan of Action vs The Berg Report: Contemporary Issues in African Economic Development* (Lawrenceville, VA: Brunswick Publishers: 1984).
4. Adedeji, Terbia, and Bugembe, *The Challenge of African Economic Recovery and Development,* 132.
5. Ibid., 133–34.
6. Ibid.
7. Ibid.
8. Ibid.
9. African Charter for Popular Participation in Development and Transformation. Arusha, Tanzania. February 12 to 16, 1990. file:///C:/Users/Thelma/AppData/Local/Packages/Microsoft.MicrosoftEdge_8wekyb3d8bbwe/TempState/Downloads/Southern_Africa_Record_Number_63.pdf.
10. www.un.org.
11. NEPAD #71.
12. S. K. B. Asante, *Implementing the New Partnership for Africa's Development (NEPAD)* (Accra, Ghana: Ghana Academy of Arts and Sciences: 2006), 2.
13. Edozie, 2004, 169.
14. Lutz, 224.
15. Lutz, 224.
16. NEPAD, 2001, 1 and 2.
17. Ravi Kanbur, "The New Partnership for Africa's Development (NEPAD): An Initial Commentary," *Politikon* 29, no. 1 (2002), 88. See original NEPAD document.
18. The New Partnership for Africa's Development (NEPAD) 2001, Section 49. http://hrlibrary.umn.edu/instree/nepad.html. Retrieved October 27, 2018.
19. Richard Joseph, "Progress and Retreat in Africa: Challenges of a Frontier," *Journal of Democracy* 19, no. 2 (2008), 96.
20. NEPAD, 2001, Section 49. http://www.nepad.org/2005/files/documents/inbrief.pdf. Retrieved July 28, 2009.
21. Ravi Kanbur, "The New Partnership for Africa's Development (NEPAD): An Initial Commentary," *Politikon* 29, no. 1 (2002), 87–100. DOI: 10.1080/0258934022014944352. Retrieved October 26, 2018.
22. NEPAD, 2001, 36.
23. Ian Taylor, "The failure of the New Economic Partnership for Africa's Development," 281. http://www.thefreelibrary.com/The+failure+of+the+New+Economic+Partnership+for+Africa's+Development.-a0102747654.
24. Elsabé Loots, "Capital Flows to the African Continent: The Development Finance Challenge" http://www.rrojasdatabank.info/widerconf/Loots.pdf. Retrieved July 5, 2014.
25. Ibid.
26. John Luiz, "The New Partnership for African Development: Africa's Response to its Underdevelopment." https://econrsa.org/system/files/publications/policy_papers_interest/pp22_interest.pdf. Retrieved July 10, 2016.
27. Ibid.
28. Ibid.

29. Rita Abrahamsen, "The Power of Partnerships in Global Governance," *Third World Quarterly* 25, no. 8 (2004): 1453–1467. https://www.jstor.org/stable/3993796?seq=1#page_scan_tab_contents. Retrieved June 8, 2015.

30. Ibid.

31. Luiz, "The New Partnership for African Development: Africa's Response to its Underdevelopment."

32. http://news.bbc.co.uk/2/hi/africa/8094401.stm, Retrieved June 27, 2009.

33. Taylor, "The failure of the New Economic Partnership for Africa's Development."

34. NEPAD, "2014–2017 Strategic Plan," NEPAD Planning and Coordinating Agency. www.http//nepad.org. Retrieved February 9, 2017.

35. Ibid.

36. Ibid.

37. "The African Charter on Democracy, Elections, and Governance." https://au.int/en/treaties/african-charter-democracy-elections-and-governance. Retrieved September 27, 2017.

38. Ibid., 3.

39. Ibid., 4.

40. Nic Cheeseman, "Why Democracy is Not Dead in Africa," *News Week*, May 25, 2017. http://www.newsweek.com/why-democracy-not-dead-africa-615368. Retrieved December 12, 2017.

41. Pierre Englebert, *Africa: Unity, Sovereignty and Sorrow* (Boulder, CO: Lynne Rienner Publishers, 2009), 219.

42. Rod Alence, "Political Institutions and Developmental Governance in Sub-Saharan Africa," *Journal of Modern African Studies* 42, no. 2 (2004), 179.

43. "Barack Obama: Africa's Future is up to Africans," *CBS News*, July 11, 2009. www.cbsnews.com/news/obama-africas-future-is up Africans?. Retrieved October 1, 2016.

Appendix A

Regression Results Based on Growth of GDP

REGRESSION RESULTS

Dependent Variable: Growth Rate of GDP Per Capita (GGDP)

	Ghana			*South Africa*		
Var.	*(1)*	*(2)*	*(3)*	*(1)*	*(2)*	*(3)*
Const.	0.020	0.010	0.012	0.140	0.036	−0.103
	(0.246)	(0.124)	(0.268)	(1.632)	(0.373)	(2.507
I/Y	−0.125	−0.103	−0.110	0.105	0.231	0.423**
	(0.284)	(0.251)	(0.341)	(0.754)	(1.541)	(4.663)
GPOP	−0.006	0.247	0.255	−0.996	1.162	2.648
	(−0.004)	(0.185)	(0.197)	(0.626)	(0.632)	(1.638)
G/Y	−0.072	0.008	. . .	−0.497*	−0.334	. . .
	(0.291)	(0.031)	(2.381)	(1.586)		
F	. . .	−0.105*	−0.104*	. . .	0.017	0.024
		(2.688)	(2.731)		(1.196)	(1.691)
NF	. . .	−0.010	−0.010	. . .	−0.037*	−0.043*
		(0.402)	(0.463)		(2.258)	(2.613)
R^2	0.003	0.190	0.190	0.416	0.511	0.472
F	0.032	1.502	1.936	8.089	6.676	7.378
DW	1.987	2.342	2.341	1.733	1.648	1.428
N=38						

Notes: Absolute values of t-statistics are in parentheses.
Partially free (PF) is the base category.
* = Significant at .05.
** = Significant at .01.

Appendix B

Regression Results Based on GDP

REGRESSION RESULTS

Dependent Variable: Gross Domestic Product per Capita, ln (*Y/P*)

Variables	*(1)*	*(2)*	*(3)*
Constant	1.722[b]	1.634[b]	1.714[b]
	(2. 611)	(2.375)	(2.578)
Ln (I/Y)	–0.157[b]	0.166[b]	–0.155[b]
	(2.363)	(2.437)	(2.338)
Ln (P)	0.203[a]	0.219[a]	0.204[a]
	(1.632)	(1.672)	(1.626)
Ln (G/Y)	0.226[c]	–0.217[c]	–0.227[c]
	(3.303)	(3.165)	(3.283)
F	–0.0132	. . .	. . .
	(0.435)		
NF	–0.0456[a]	. . .	. . .
	(1.815)		
Ln (OP)	0.334[b]	0.341[b]	0.335[b]
	(2.565)	(2.575)	(2.554)
Ln (*G/Y*)**F*		–0.0150	. . .
		(0.536)	
ln(*G/Y*) **NF*		–0.0565[a]	. . .
		(1.598)	
ln (*OP*)**F*			0.0060
			(0.401)
ln(*OP*)**NF*			–0.0251[a]
			(1.742)
R^2	0.398	0.385	0.393
F	4.958[c]	13.849[c]	3.563[c]
N = 40.			

Notes: Absolute values of t-statistics are in parentheses. NF (not free) is the base category.
a = Significant at 0.10.
b = Significant at 0.05.
c = Significant at 0.01.

Appendix C

AGOA Apparel Rules

SUMMARY OF APPAREL RULES OF ORIGIN UNDER AGOA

Description of the Rules of Origin Requirements	*Conditions of Access*
Apparel assembled from US formed and cut fabric from US yarn	Unrestricted
Apparel assembled and further processed from US formed and cut fabric from US yarn	Unrestricted
Apparel cut and assembled from US fabric from US yarn and thread	Unrestricted
Apparel assembled from regional fabric from US or African yarn	Tariff rate quota that grows from 1.5% to 3.5% of total US apparel imports
Apparel assembled in a lesser developed country using foreign fabric or yarn	Unrestricted for four years, but exports counted against the 1.5–3.5% caps
	Specified above
Cashmere sweaters, knit to shape	Unrestricted
Merino wool sweater, knit to shape, with fibers 18.5 microns or finer	Unrestricted

Source: Aaditya Mattoo, Davesh Roy, and Arvind Subramanian. "The Africa Growth and Opportunity Act and Its Rules of Origin: Generosity Undermined?" *World Economy* 26, no. 6 (2003), 837.

Appendix D

AGOA Eligibility

AGOA Eligible Countries, the Effective Date of Eligibility, and the Effective Date of Eligibility for AGOA Apparel Benefits if Applicable*

	Country	*Date Declared AGOA Eligible*	*Date Declared Eligible for Apparel Provision*	*Special Rules for Apparel*
1.	Angola	December 30, 2003		
2.	Benin	October 2, 2000	January 28, 2004	Yes
3.	Botswana	October 2, 2000	August 27, 2001	Yes
4.	Burkina Faso	December 10, 2004	August 4, 2006	Yes
5.	Burundi	January 1, 2006		
6.	Cameroon	October 2, 2000	March 1, 2002	Yes
7.	Cape Verde	October 2, 2000	August 28, 2002	Yes
8.	Chad	October 2, 2000	April 26, 2006	Yes
9.	Comoros	July 1, 2008		
10.	Congo	October 2, 2000		
11.	Democratic Republic of Congo*	December 31, 2002		
12.	Djibouti			
13.	Ethiopia	October 2, 2000	August 2, 2001	Yes
14.	Gabon	October 2, 2000	March 20, 2002	No
15.	Gambia	December 31, 2002		
16.	Ghana	October 2, 2000		
17.	Guinea	October 2, 2000		
18.	Guinea-Bissau	October 2, 2000		
19.	Kenya	October 2, 2000	January 18, 2001	
20.	Lesotho	October 2, 2000	April 23, 2001	
21.	Liberia	December 29, 2006		

(*Continued*)

	Country	*Date Declared AGOA Eligible*	*Date Declared Eligible for Apparel Provision*	*Special Rules for Apparel*
22.	Madagascar	October 2, 2000	March 6, 2001	Yes
23.	Malawi	October 2, 2000	August 15, 2001	Yes
24.	Mali	October 2, 2000	December 11, 2003	Yes
25.	Mauritania	June 2007		
26.	Mauritius	October 2, 2000	January 18, 2001	No
27.	Mozambique	October 2, 2000	February 8, 2002	Yes
28.	Namibia	October 2, 2000	December 3, 2001	Yes
29.	Niger	October 2, 2000	December 17, 2003	Yes
30.	Nigeria	October 2, 2000	July 14, 2004	Yes
31.	Rwanda	October 2, 2000	March 4, 2003	Yes
32.	Sao Tome and Principe	October 2, 2000		

*AGOA trade preferences granted on October 31, 2003.
Source: African Growth and Opportunity Act. http://www.agoa.gov.

Appendix E

US Trade with Sub-Saharan African Countries in 2016

2016 U.S. TOTAL TRADE with sub-Saharan Africa		
Value (in millions)	% Change from 2014	% of Total Trade with World
$33,733	-8.46%	0.93%

2016 U.S. EXPORTS to sub-Saharan Africa				
Value (in millions)	% Change from 2014	% of Total Exports to World	Drivers of Decrease in Exports to SSA	
$13,602	-24.48%	0.94%	-39% Oil; -38% vehicles; -32% Civilian aircraft & parts; -31% Machinery	
Top 5 SSA Destinations for U.S. Exports				
OUNTRY	VALUE (in millions)	% of Total to SSA	% Change from 2014	Top Commodities
South Africa	4,685.29	34.45%	-14.16%	Machinery; Vehicles & parts; Electrical machinery; Civilian aircraft & parts; Medical Instruments
Nigeria	1,875.38	13.79%	-45.45%	Machinery; Vehicles; Cereals (wheat & meslin)
Angola	1,275.76	9.38%	9.40%	Aircraft & parts; Machinery; Electrical machinery
Ghana	830.49	6.11%	-12.57%	Vehicles; Machinery; Electr machinery; Aircraft/parts
Ethiopia	827.29	6.08%	-46.81%	Civilian aircraft & parts; Cereals (wheat & meslin)

2016 U.S. IMPORTS from sub-Saharan Africa				
Value (in millions)	% Change from 2014	% of Total Exports to World	Drivers of Increase in Imports from SSA	
$20,132	6.85%	0.92%	+23% Mineral fuel; +12% Cocoa; +8% Precious stones	
Top 5 SSA Sources of U.S. Imports				
COUNTRY	VALUE (in millions)	% of Total from SSA	% Change from 2014	Top Commodities
South Africa	6,759.20	33.57%	-7.59%	Platinum/diamonds; Vehicles & parts; Iron & steel;
Nigeria	4,175.99	20.74%	117.98%	Oil (crude)
Angola	2,856.48	14.19%	1.78%	Oil (crude); Diamonds
Côte d'Ivoire	1,163.92	5.78%	13.23%	Cocoa; Rubber; Cashew nuts
Chad	898.68	4.46%	-31.05%	Oil (crude)

2016 U.S. AGOA IMPORTS from sub-Saharan Africa					
Value (in millions)		% Change from 2014	% of Total Imports from SSA		
$10.58		+14.2%	53%		
Top 5 SSA Sources of U.S. AGOA Imports			**Top 5 AGOA Sectors**		
COUNTRY	VALUE (in millions)	% Change from 2015	Sector	VALUE (in millions)	% Change from 2014
Nigeria	$3,478	+147%%	Energy-related	$6,415	25%
South Africa	$2,846	-0.4%	Transp. Equip	$1,651	8%
Angola	$1,956	-7%	Textiles/apparel	$1,009	2%
Chad	$775	-48%	Minerals/metals	$545	-10%
Kenya	$395	-9%	Ag products	$488	1%

Source: AGOA International Trade Administration, June 5, 2017. https://www.trade.gov/agoa/pdf/2016%20US-SSA%20Trade%20One-Pager.pdf.

Bibliography

108th United States Congress. 2004. H.R. 4103 AGOA Acceleration Act of 2004, edited by Congress of the United States.

Abacha, Sani. 1994. "Domestic Policy." *Nigerian Economist* 7 (31): 1–2.

Aborisade, O. and R. J. Mundt. 2002. *Politics in Nigeria.* New York, NY: Longman Publishers.

Acemoglu, Daron, Suresh Naidu, James Robinson, and Pascual Restrepo. 2014. "Does Democracy Boost Economic Growth?" *VOX CEPR Policy Portal.*

Acemoglu, Daron, Suresh Naidu, Pascual Restrepo, and James A. Robinson. 2014. "Democracy Does Cause Growth." *National Bureau of Economic Research Working Paper Series*, no. 20004. doi: 10.3386/w20004.

Adedji, Adebayo, Teriba Owodunni, and Patrick Bugembe. 1991. *The Challenge of African Economic Recovery and Development.* London: Frank Cass Publisher.

African Union. "The African Charter on Democracy, Elections, and Governance." https://au.int/en/treaties/african-charter-democracy-elections-and-governance. Retrieved September 27, 2017.

AGOA. "African Growth and Opportunity Act." https://agoa.info/about-agoa/country-eligibility.html.

Agwa, Ichechukwu. 2004. *Legal Opinion on Section 419 Criminal Code Laws of Nigeria.* Unpublished edition. Lagos, Nigeria: Rhodes & Rhodes, Barristers, Solicitors & Notaries Public.

Akech, Migai. 2001. "The African Growth and Opportunity Act: Implications for Kenya's Trade and Development," *New York Journal of International Law and Politics* 32: 651–53.

Alence, R. 2004. "Political Institutions and Developmental Governance in Sub-Saharan Africa." *Journal of Modern African Studies* 42 (2): 163–87.

Almukhtar, Sarah, K. K. Rebecca Lai, Sergio Pecanha, Derek Watkins, and Jeremy White. 2015. "What's Behind the Surge in Refugees Crossing the Mediterranean Sea," *New York Times.* Accessed September 5, 2015. https://www.nytimes.com/interactive/2015/04/20/world/europe/surge-in-refugees-crossing-the-mediterranean-sea-maps.html?_r=0.

Amuzie, Eme, Godfrey Ikhemuemhe, and Martins Azukiew. May 2, 1994. "No Way Out" 7 (31), 12, cited in Guseh, James S. 1997. "Government Size and Economic Growth in Developing Countries: A Political-Economy Framework," *Journal of Macroeconomics* 19 (1), 175–92. doi: https://doi.org/10.1016/S0164-0704(97)00010-4.

Ankomah, Baffour. "High Noon in Zimbabwe," *New African*, May 2008.

Anonymous. 2003. "Public Enterprises Indicted in N3.8 Trillion Debt." *Daily Independent*. http://www.odili.net.

Anunobi, F. O. 1992. *The Implications of Conditionality: The International Monetary Fund and Africa*. Landham, MD: University Press of America.

Asante, S. K. B. 2006. *Implementing the new Partnership for Africa's Development (NEPAD)*. Accra, Ghana: Ghana Academy of Arts and Sciences.

Asante, W. and E. B. Asare. 2015. "Ghana's 2012 Election Petition and Its Outcome: A Giant Leap towards Democratic Consolidation." *Journal of Political Sciences & Public Affairs* 4 (1): 1–6.

Azam, J. P., A. Fosu, and N. S. Ndung'u. 2002. *Explaining Slow Growth in Africa*. Malden, MA: Blackwell Publishers.

Bairam, Erkin. 1990. "Government Size and Economic Growth: The African Experience, 1960–85." *Applied Economics* 22 (10): 1427–35. doi: 10.1080/00036849000000113.

Barro, Robert J. 1991. "Economic Growth in a Cross Section of Countries*." *The Quarterly Journal of Economics* 106 (2): 407–43. doi: 10.2307/2937943.

BBC Africa. 2016. "Ghana Election: Opposition Leader Akufo-Addo Declared Winner." https://www.bbc.com/news/world-africa-38270956. Retrieved February 17, 2017.

BBC News. 2006. "No Third Term for Nigerian Leader." accessed December 2, 2008. http://news.bbc.co.uk/2/hi/africa/4986904.stm.

BBC News. 2015. "Nigeria Election: Muhammadu Buhari Wins Presidency." https://www.bbc.com/news/world-africa-32139858.

Bennell, Paul. 1997. "Foreign Direct Investment in Africa: Rhetoric and Reality." *SAIS Review* 17 (2): 127–127.

Berry, Brian J. L., Edgar C. Conkling, and D. Michael Ray. 1992. *The Global Economy: Resource Use, Locational Choice, and International Trade*. Englewood Cliffs, NJ: Prentice Hall.

Birmingham, David. "Central African Republic." accessed November 3. http://www.britannica.com/EBchecked/topic/102127/Central-Africa.

Boafo-Arthur, Kwame. 1999. "Ghana: Structural Adjustment, Democratization, and the Politics of Continuity." *African Studies Review* 42 (2): 41–72. doi: 10.2307/525364.

Bolaji, Mohammed H. A. 2013. "Between Democracy and Federalism: Shari'ah in Northern Nigeria and the Paradox of Institutional Impetuses." *Africa Today* 59 (4): 93–117. doi: 10.2979/africatoday.59.4.93.

Browne, Robert S. and Robert J. Cummings. 1984. *The Lagos Plan of Action vs The Berg Report: Contemporary Issues ion African Economic Development*. Lawrenceville, VA: Brunswick Publishers.

Campbell, John. 2012. "Nigeria's Battle for Stability." *The National Interest* (118): 31–39.

Carr, Dara. 2004. "Improving the health of the world's poorest people." In *Health Bulletin*. Washington, DC: Population Reference Bureau.

CBS News. 2009. "Obama: 'Africa's Future Is Up to Africans'." accessed October 1, 2016. https://www.cbsnews.com/news/obama-africas-future-is-up-to-africans/.

Charles A. Whittier. 1998. "The African Growth and Opportunity Act: A Cup Half Empty or Half Full?" *Black Business Journal* 1–5. http:www.bbjonline.com/archives.

Cheeseman, Nic. 2017. "Why Democracy is Not Dead in Africa." *Newsweek.*

CIA Factbook. "Algeria." https://www.cia.gov/library/publications/the-world-factbook/geos/ag.html.

CIA Factbook. "Central African Republic." https://www.cia.gov/library/publications/resources/the-world-factbook/geos/ct.html.

CIA Factbook. "Nigeria." https://www.cia.gov/library/publications/the-world-factbook/geos/ni.html#top.

Collier, Paul and Jan Willem Gunning. 1999. "Explaining African Economic Performance." *Journal of Economic Literature* 37 (1): 64–111.

Commander, Simon, John Howell, and Wayo Siena. 1989. "Ghana: 1983–1987." In *Structural Adjustment & Agriculture: Theory and Practice in Africa and Latin America*, edited by Simon Commander. London: Overseas Development Institute.

Devarajan, Shantayanan, William R. Easterly, and Howard Pack. 2003. "Low Investment is Not the Constraint on African Development." *Economic Development and Cultural Change* 51 (3): 547–71. doi: 10.1086/368154.

Diamond, Larry. 2008. "Progress and Retreat in Africa: The Rule of Law versus the Big Man." *Journal of Democracy* 19 (2): 138–49.

Dugger, Celia W. and Barry Bearak. 2008. "Mugabe is Sworn in to Sixth Term After Victory in One-Candidate Runoff." *New York Times*. https://www.nytimes.com/2008/06/30/world/africa/30zimbabwe.html. Retrieved November 16, 2008.

Dumas, Lloyd. 1999. "Democratization and Demilitarization: Building Peace and Prosperity in Africa." *Developmental Policy Studies, The Newsletter Journal of the National PSO's* 5 (1): 13–20.

Easterly, William. 2000. "The Joys and Sorrows of Openness: A Review Essay." In *The Determinants of Economic Growth*, edited by M. S. Oosterbaan, Thijs De Ruyter Van Steveninck and N. Van Der Windt, 39–73. Boston, MA: Springer US.

Englebert, Pierre. 2009. *Africa: Unity, Sovereignty and Sorrow*. Boulder, Colorado: Lynne Rienner Publisher.

Fergusson, I. F. and L. M. Sek. 2003. *US Trade and Investment Relationship with Sub-Saharan Africa: The African Growth and Opportunity Act and Beyond*. Washington, DC: Congressional Research Services.

Fisher-Thompson, J. 2002. "Africa: A Top Policy Priority in the New Bush Strategy Plan." *US Foreign Policy Agenda, An Electronic Journal of the US Department of State* 7 (4): 28–31.

Fithin, Caspar. 2000. "Nigeria - Rapacious Corruption." *Oxford Analytical Weekly*, Column 1–4.

Folasade-Koyi, m Adetutu. 2003. "Public Enterprises Indicted in N3.8 Trillion Debt." *Daily Independent Online*.
Freedom House. *Freedom in the World: Country Ratings 1972–2005*. Washington, DC. Freedom House online sub-Saharan report. http://freedomhouse. org/regions/ sub-sahara. Retrieved on September 11, 2006.
Freedom House. "Sub-Saharan Africa," Freedom House online report. https:// freedomhouse.org/regions/sub-saharan-africa. Retrieved September 11, 2016.
Freedom House. "Zimbabwe," Freedom House online report. https://freedomhouse. org/report/freedom-world/2016/zimbabwe. Retrieved September 9, 2016.
Freedom House. 1973. "The New Criteria of Freedom." *Freedom at Issue* 17: 2–23.
Freedom House. 2012. *Freedom in the World: Ethiopa*. Freedom House: Washington, DC.
Freedom House. 2016. *Freedom in the World: Cameroon*. Freedom House: Washington, DC.
Freedom House. May 2, 2007. "Press Freedom Findings in Middle East and North Africa Disappointing after Earlier Hopeful Years." *Freedom House*. https:// freedomhouse.org/article/press-freedom-findings-middle-east-and-north-africa-disappointing-after-earlier-hopeful.
International Monetary Fund. 2009. *The Multilateral Debt Relief Initiative*. Retrieved from https://www.imf.org/external/np/ext/facts/mdri.htm on October 22, 2018.
Gallagher, Mary E. 2011. "'Reform and Openness': Why China's Economic Reforms Have Delayed Democracy." *World Politics* 54 (3): 338–72. doi: 10.1353/wp.2002.0009.
Gastil, Raymond. 1973. "Freedom in the World." *Freedom at Issue* 17: 2–23.
Geviser, M. 2009. "Time of Reckoning." *BBC Focus on Africa Magazine* 20 (2): 18.
Gibbon, Peter. 2003. "The African Growth and Opportunity Act and the Global Commodity Chain for Clothing." *World Development* 31 (11): 1809–27. doi: https://doi.org/10.1016/j.worlddev.2003.06.002.
Global Edge. "Central Africa Region Political History." http://globaledge.msu.edu/ Countries/Central-African-Republic/History.
Guseh, James S. 1997. "Government Size and Economic Growth in Developing Countries: A Political-Economy Framework." *Journal of Macroeconomics* 19 (1): 175–92. doi: https://doi.org/10.1016/S0164-0704(97)00010-4.
Gyimah, Boadi E. 2001. "A Peaceful Turnover in Ghana." *Journal of Democracy* 12 (2): 103–117.
Heston, Alan, Robert Summers, and Bettina Aten. 2009. "Penn World TableVersion 6.3." accessed May 27, 2003. http://datacentre.chass.utoronto.ca/pwt/.
Hinshaw, Drew. June 25, 2015. "US-Africa Trade Gets a Boost With Renewal of AGOA." *Frontier Markets*, September 13, 2015.
Hirshleifer, J. 1991. "The Paradox of Power." *Economics and Politics* 3 (3): 177–200.
Ho-Wong, Jeong. 1998. "Economic Reform and Democratic Transition in Ghana." *World Affairs* 160 (4): 218–31.
Hoekman, Bernard, Francis Ng, and Marcelo Olarreaga. May 2002. "Eliminating Excessive Tariffs on Exports of Least Developed Countries." *The World Bank Economic Reviews* 16 (1): 19.
Hoekstra, Pete. 2016. "Buhari is Nigeria's Problem, Not Its Solution. It's Hard to see How President Buhari's Policies are Good for Nigeria's Future." *Wall Street*

Journal. https://www.wsj.com/articles/buhari-is-nigerias-problem-not-its-solution-1466109183.
Hutchful, Eboe. 1997. "Reconstructing Civil Military Relations and the Collapse of Democracy in Ghana, 1979–81." *African Affairs* 96 (385): 535–60.
International Conference on Popular Participation in the, Recovery, and Africa DevelopmentProcessin. 1990. *African charter for popular participation in development and transformation (Arusha 1990)*: [s.n.] UNECA.
International Crisis Group. 2012. *Implementing Peace and Security Architecture (II): Southern Africa*. Retrieved from: https://www.crisisgroup.org/africa/southern-africa/implementing-peace-and-security-architecture-ii-southern-africa on October 24, 2018.
International Trade Administration. 2016. "Summary of AGOA I." http://trade.gov/agoa/legislation/index.asp.
Jeong, Byeongju. 2002. "Policy Uncertainty and Long-Run Investment and Output Across Countries." *International Economic Review* 43 (2): 363–92.
Jeong, H. 1998. "Economic Reform and Democratic Transition in Ghana." *World Affairs* 160 (4): 218–31.
Joseph, Richard. 2008. "Challenges of Frontier Region." *Journal of Democracy* 19 (2): 2–16.
Jreisat, Jamil. 2012. *Globalism and Comparative Public Administration*. New York: CRC Press.
Kaba, Amadu Jacky. 2004. "Africa-U.S. Partnership in the 21st Century." *Chimera: US African Instutite* 2 (1): 15–25.
Kanbur, R. 2002. "The New Partnership for Africa's Development (NEPAD): An Initial Commentary." *Politikon* 29 (1): 87–100.
Keller, E. J. and D. Rothchild. 1996. *Africa in the New International Order*. Boulder, Colorado: Lynne Reinner Publishers.
Honorable Uhuru Kenyatta's "Speech by the Incoming of he AGOA African Consultative Group" Kenya Office of the Deputy Prime Minister and Ministry of Trade. July 14, 2008. Retrieved at http://democracyafrica.org/agoacsonet/kenyaopm2008.
Kraay, Aart Zoido-Lobaton Pablo Kaufmann Daniel. 1999. *Governance Matters, Policy Research Working Papers: The World Bank*. doi: 10.1596/1813-9450-2196.
Lemarchand, Rene. 2001. "Foreign Policy Making in the Great Lakes Region." In *African Foreign Policies: Power and Process*, edited by Gilbert Khadiagala and Terrence Lyons. Boulder, CO: Lynne Rienner Publishers.
Luckham, R. 1971. *The Nigerian Military: A Sociological Analysis of Authority and Revolt*. Cambridge, UK: Cambridge University.
Maiangwa, Benjamin, Ufo Okeke Uzodike, Ayo Whetho, and Hakeem Onapajo. 2012. "Baptism by Fire: Boko Haram and the Reign of Terror in Nigeria." *Africa Today* 59 (2): 40–57.
Martin, W. 1998. "Dictated Trade: The Case Against the African Growth and Opportunity Act." *Review of African Political Economy* 27 (77): 531–32.
Mates, Robert. 2002. "South Africa: Democracy Without the People." *Journal of Democracy* 13 (1): 23–26.

Mattoo, A., D. Roy, and A. Subramanian. 2003. "The Africa Growth and Opportunity Act and Its Rules of Origin: Generosity Undermined." *World Economy* 26 (6): 829–51.

Mbaku, M. 2003. "Entrenching Economic Freedom in Africa." *The Cato Journal* 23 (2): 217–25.

Mo Ibrahim Foundation. 2016. *2016 Ibrahim Index of African Governance: A Decade of African Governance 2006–2015*. MoIbrahim Foundation.

Moyo, Dambisa. 2009. *Dead Aid: Why Aid is Not Working and How There is a Better Way for Africa*. Vancover, BCV: Douglas & McIntyre.

Nationmaster. 2003. "Nigerian Economy Profile." accessed October 27, 2003. http://www.nationmaster.com/country-info/profiles/Nigeria/Economy.

Nbuchu, D. 1993. "The Looting of Nigeria." *African Guardian*.

Office of the United States Trade Representative. "Preference Programs." accessed October 25, 2008. https://ustr.gov/issue-areas/preference-programs.

Office of the United States Trade Representative. August 2017. *Opening Statement of USTR Robert Lighthizer at 2017 AGOA Forum*. Washington, DC: Office of the United States Trade Representative.

Oko, O. 2002. "Subverting the Scourge of Corruption in Nigeria: A Reform Prospectus." *New York University Journal of International Law & Politics* 34: 397–474.

Olaitan, W. 1995. "The State and Economy in Nigeria: A Conceptualization." In *The Political Economy of Nigeria Under the Military Rule 1984–1993*, edited by Said Adejumobi and Momoh Abubakar. Harare, Zimbabwe: SAPES Books.

Olukoshi, A. 1993. *The Politics of Structural Adjustment in Nigeria*. Ibadan: Heinemann Educational Books.

Olukoshi, A. 1995. "The Political Economy of Structural Adjustment Program." In *The Political Economy of Nigeria Under the Military Rule 1984–1993,* edited by Said Adejumobi and Momoh Abubakar. Harare, Zimbabwe: SAPES Books.

Omede, A. J. 2011. "Nigerian: Analyzing the Security Challenges of the Goodluck Jonathan Administration." *Canadian Social Science* 7 (5): 90–102.

Omonobi, Kingsley. 2015. "Why Buhari Axed Service Chiefs Ahead of US Visit!" *Vanguard*. accessed July 19, 2005. https://www.vanguardngr.com/2015/07/why-buhari-axed-service-chiefs-ahead-of-us-visit/.

Onuorah, Madu. 2003. "Government Spends N92 Billion on Debt Servicing in 10 Months." *The Guardian Newspaper*. http://www.Odili.net.

Organization of African Unity. "Organization of African Unity." accessed October 10, 2017. http://www.dirco.gov.za/foreign/Multilateral/africa/oau.htm.

Organization of African Unity. 2000. *Constitutive Act of the African Union*. Lome, Togo: Organization of African Unity, July 1, 2000.

Osayimwese, Izevbuwa and Sunday Iyare. 1991. "The Economics of Nigerian Federalism: Selected Issues in Economic Management." *Publius: The Journal of Federalism* 21 (4): 89–101. doi: 10.1093/oxfordjournals.pubjof.a037981.

Osborne, Evan. 2004. "Measuring Bad Governance." *The Cato Journal* 23 (3): 402–22.

Otobo, Dafe. 1986. "Bureaucratic Elites and Public-Sector Wage Bargaining in Nigeria." *The Journal of Modern African Studies* 24 (1): 101–26.

Perkins, Dwight H., Malcolm Gillis, Steven C. Radelet, Donald R. Snodgrass, and Michael Roemer. 2001. *Economics of Development*, fifth edition. New York, NY: W.W. Norton & Company.

Peters, Guy B. 2015. *American Public Policy: Promise and Performance*, tenth edition. Los Angeles, California: CQ Press.

Plümper, Thomas and Christian W. Martin. 2003. "Democracy, Government Spending, and Economic Growth: A Political-Economic Explanation of the Barro-Effect." *Public Choice* 117 (1): 27–50. doi: 10.1023/A:1026112530744.

Posner, Daniel N. and Daniel J. Young. 2007. "The Institutionalization of Political Power in Africa." *Journal of Democracy* 18 (3): 126–40.

Prabhakara, M. S. January 20–February 2, 2001. "A History of Coups." *Frontline* 18 (2): 1–5.

Prayer, C. 1989. "Causes of the Debt Crisis." In *The IMF, The World Bank and the African Debt: The Economic Impact*, vol. 1, edited by Bade Onimade. London: Zed Books.

Puddington, Arch. "Essay: Freedom Stagnation Amid Pushback Against Democracy," *Freedom in the World 2007*, Freedom House online report. Freedom House online report. https://freedomhouse.org/report/freedom-world-2007/essay-freedom-stagnation-amid-pushback-against-democracy.

Raftopoulos, Brian and Ian Phimister. 2004. "Zimbabwe Now: The Political Economy of Crisis and Coercion." *Historical Materialism* 12 (4): 355–82.

Ram, Rati. 1986. "Government Size and Economic Growth: A New Framework and Some Evidence from Cross-Section and Time-Series Data." *The American Economic Review* 76 (1): 191–203.

Reviser, Mark. 2009. "Time of Reckoning." *BBC Focus*.

Ross, Will. 2015. "Nigeria Election: Muhammadu Buhari Wins Presidency." https://www.bbc.com/news/av/world-africa-32142991/nigeria-election-muhammadu-buhari-wins-presidency.

Rubin, Leslie and Brian Weinstein. 1977. *Introduction to African Politics*. New York, NY: Holt Publishing Company.

Sach, J. D. 2012. "From Millennium Goals to Sustainable Development Goals." *Lanct View Points* 379: 2206–11.

Sachikonye, Lloyd M. 2002. "Whither Zimbabwe? crisis & democratisation." *Review of African Political Economy* 29 (91): 13–20. doi: 10.1080/03056240208704581.

Santiso, Carlos. 2001. "Good Governance and Aid Effectiveness: The World Bank and Conditionality," *The Georgetown Public Policy Review* 7 (1): 1–22.

Schneidman, W. 1990. "President Clinton's Partnership Initiative." *Economic Perspectives* 4 (3): 11–13.

Scully, Gerald W. 1988. *The Institutional Framework and Economic Development*, vol. 96.

Sklar, Richard, Ebere Onwudiwe, and Darren Kew. 2096. "Nigeria: Completing Obasanjo's Legacy." *Journal of Political Economy* 17 (3): 2, 100–15.

Slater, R. 1999. "Promoting Trade and Investment in Africa." *Economic Perspectives* 4 (3): 3–5.

Smith, Adam. 1776. *An Inquiry into the Nature and Causes of the Wealth of Nations*. London: Methuen & Company.

Smith, Daniel. 2002. "Ghana's 2000 Elections: Consolidating Multiparty Democracy." *Electoral Studies* 21 (3): 519–26.

Soyinka, Wole. 2012. *The Butchers of Nigeria: How a Corrupt Nation Bred Boko Haram, the Islamic Sect Terrorizing the Country's Christians*. New York: Newsweek Media Group, Inc.

Suberu, Rotimi T. 2001. "Can Nigeria's New Democracy Survive?" *Current History* 100 (646): 207–12.

Swarnajothi, S. 2009. "Good Governance, Public Accountability and Audit." http://www.asosai.org/system/upload_file/assembly/20100129094411 1.pdf.

Taylor, Ian. 2014. "The Failure of the New Economic Partnership for Africa's Development." https://www.thefreelibrary.com/The+failure+of+the+New+Economic+Partnership+for+Africa's+Development.-a0102747654. Retrieved September 27, 2017.

Thompson, Nicholas. 2009. "You've Got Fraud." http://foreignpolicy.com/2009/11/03/youve-got-fraud/.

Transparency International. 2014. "Corruption Perceptions Index 2014: Results." In *Global Regional and Country Reports*. https://www.transparency.org/cpi2014/resultstransparencyinternational.

Trent, R. 2002. "Implications for Foreign Direct Investment in Sub-Saharan Africa und the African Growth and Opportunity Act." *Northwestern Journal of International Law & Business* 123 (1): 213–37.

United Nations Conference on Trade and Development. 2003. *World Investment Report, 2003, FDI Policies for Development: National and International Perspective*. New York and Geneva: United Nations.

United Nations Development Programme. "Millenium Development Goals." *United Nations Development Programme*. http://www.undp.org/content/undp/en/home/sdgoverview/mdg_goals.html. Retrieved February 18, 2009.

United Nations Economic Commission for Africa. *Harmonization of Mining Policies, Standards, Legislative and Regulatory Frameworks in Southern Africa*. Southern Africa Office. https://www.uneca.org/publications/harmonization-mining-policies-standards-legislative-and-regulatory-frameworks-southern. Retrieved October 24, 2018.

United Nations ESCAP. 2009. "What is Good Governance?" http://www.unescap.org/pdd/prs/ProjectActivities/Ongoing/gg/governance.asp. Retrieved May 28, 2012.

United States Department of Commerce. 2007. *International Trade Administration*. Washington, DC, 2007. http://www.agoa.gov/resources/US-African%20Trade%20Profile%2 02008%20-%20Final.pdf. Retrieved March 14, 2009.

Vesely, M. 2003. "AGOA - The Nuts and Bolts." *African Business* (January 2003), (247): 30–32.

Vunyingah, Michael. March 2011. "Unconstitutional Changes of Government in Africa: An Assessment of the Relevance of the Constitutive Act of the African Union." *Policy Brief Africa Institute of South Africa*, Briefing No. 44.

Weiss, Thomas G. 2000. "Governance, Good Governance and Global Governance: Conceptual and Actual Challenges." *Third World Quarterly* 21 (5): 795–814.

Whitaker, Rosa. November 20, 2012. "The Obameter: Strengthen the African Growth and Opportunity Act." *Politifact*. https://www.politifact.com/truth-o-meter/promises/obameter/promise/429/strengthen-the-african-growth-and-opportunity-act/.

WhiteHouse. July 13, 2004. *To Take Certain Actions Under the African Growth and Opportunity Act*. Washington, DC: Office of the Press Secretary.

Whittier, C. A. 1998. "The African Growth and Opportunity Act: A Cup Half Empty or Half Full?" *Black Business Journal*, 1–5.

Wonkeryor, Edward Lama, Ella Forbes, and James S. Guseh. 2000. *American Democracy in Africa in the Twenty-First Century?* Cherry Hill, NJ: Africana Homestead Legacy Publishers.

World Bank. "World Development Indicators 2003." http://documents.worldbank.org/curated/en/973231468331252903/World-development-indicators-2003.

World Economic Forum. "Five Factors Limiting the Impact of BRICS Nations." https://www.weforum.org/agenda/2015/07/5-factors-limiting-the-impact-of-the-brics-nations/.

World Economic Forum. 2014. "Agenda: The Stories Shaping the Global, Regional, and Industry Agendas." http://weforum.org/agenda.

Index

Page references for figures and tables are italicized

About the Authors

James S. Guseh is professor of political economy, law, and public administration at North Carolina Central University. He has taught at other institutions, including the University of Liberia, State University of New York (Fredonia), and Shaw University.

He has lived and worked in Liberia, where he served as a legal advisor and senior economist in the Ministry of Finance and as Assistant Minister of Justice for Economic Affairs. He has worked as consultant for the United Nations Development Programme on governance and natural resource development in several West African countries.

He has numerous publications including a coauthored book entitled American Democracy in Africa. His other publications have appeared in *Journal of African Policy Studies*, *African Social Science Review*, *Journal of Diplomacy and International Relations*, *The Encyclopedia of Public Administration and Public Policy*, *Journal of Macroeconomics*, *Public Integrity*, *Presidential Studies Quarterly*, *Journal of Public Management and Social Policy*, *Journal of Public Scholarship in Higher Education*, University Partnerships for International Development, and *Third World Studies Journal.*

He received BA in economics from Brandeis University, MS in Economics from the University of Oregon, the joint JD-MPA in Law and Public Administration from Syracuse University, and MA and PhD in Political Economy from the University of Texas at Dallas. He also completed studies at The Hague Academy of International Law in the Netherlands.

Emmanuel O. Oritsejafor received his MA and PhD in Political Science from Clark-Atlanta University. He is professor of political science at North Carolina Central University-Durham, North Carolina. His teaching and research interests include political economy, comparative politics, international relations, and public policy. He has worked as a consultant for the United Nations Development Program in Liberia on public service delivery and with the Liberian Legislature on the development of Minimum Wage Policy in Liberia.

He has published numerous articles in journals and book chapters. His areas of teaching and research are comparative politics, public policy, development administration, and political economy of developing states. He has published in the following academic research journals:

African Quarterly, the African Social Science Review, Journal of African Policy Studies, Journal of College and Character, Journal of Commonwealth Youth and Development, The Encyclopedia of Public Administration and Public Policy Studies, Journal of Global Competitiveness, Liberian Studies Journal, Journal of Public Management and Social Policy, The Journal of Pan African Studies Journal of Sustainable Development in Africa, the Journal of Safety and Crisis Management, Third World Studies Journal, and *Whitehead Journal of Diplomacy and International Relations.*

Lightning Source UK Ltd.
Milton Keynes UK
UKHW041513140219
337169UK00007B/481/P

9 781498 532990